# ST ALBION
# PARISH NEWS

## BOOK 7

Published in Great Britain by
Private Eye Productions Ltd, 6 Carlisle Street, W1D 3BN.
© 2004 Pressdram Ltd
ISBN 1 901784 35 5
Designed by Bridget Tisdall
Printed in England by Goodman Baylis Ltd, Worcester
2 4 6 8 10 9 7 5 3 1

# The Vicar Digs In!

# ST ALBION PARISH NEWS
# BOOK 7

Further letters from the vicar,
the Rev. A.R.P. Blair MA (Oxon)

compiled for

# PRIVATE EYE

by Ian Hislop, Richard Ingrams,
Christopher Booker and Barry Fantoni

# *Thought for the Year*

## The Vicar's not for turning

*(Gospel according to St Margaret, 19.90)*

# ST ALBION PARISH NEWS

*3rd October 2003*

*Hullo!*

And thank you all for making this year's annual parish outing to Bournemouth such a great success.

And what wonderful weather we had for it! It makes all the difference, doesn't it, when the weather is nice? Strolling along the front, watching all my friends from the Working Men's Club eating their fish 'n' chips – my favourite meal by the way.

And thank goodness everyone heeded my plea not to bring up silly topics that no one is interested in that all happened long ago – such as, Mr Hutton, Dr Kelly, the Rev. Dubya and all that boring war stuff!

We all know that what really matters is that we should sort out what's going on in our own parish, before worrying about things which don't really concern us, such as Iraq!

So let's focus on what's been going on here in St Albion's, shall we? And I don't mean Mr Hutton sitting there in the parish hall raking over a lot of dead ashes!

Do we really care about what Mr Campbell said to Mr Hoon about poor Dr Walter Mitty? Or what Mr Campbell wrote in his diary about Mr Scarlett and Mr Gilligan?

Of course we don't! It's all water under the bridge!!

Let's hope we can all now concentrate on what is really important – ie, supporting your vicar so that he can support you!

As it says in the Good Book, "I am thy Vicar and thou shalt have no other vicar but me"! (*Book of Exodus*, but only in my own good time!)

Yours,

Tony

PS. I am told that poor Dr Mitty had quite a history of suicide in his family, so those people who are going around saying that I am to blame for his death should examine their consciences!

Whatever Mr Hutton may say (and, frankly, who cares?), it is now quite obvious that poor Dr Mitty had only himself to blame for his unfortunate death (along, of course, possibly, with Mr Hoon).

# Confessions.....

■ The Vicar will not be making any confession this week because he doesn't think he's done anything wrong. Other people like Mr Hoon may well wish to confess their sins and be given the sackrement, but the Vicar has been entirely in the right all along. Anyone who wishes to see the Vicar privately to make confession can come to the vicarage between 10am-11am on a Thursday and say three "Hail Maggies". T.B.

## New Creed For Use At Mass (Destruction)

We believe in Weapons, both visible and invisible, and in the mother of all bombs, which was conceived by the Reverend Dubya and was made up on earth then (cont. p. 94)

## Also new from the Vicar
### The Nunc Di Mitty

Lord, don't lettest thou thy servant depart at all. Amen

# Harvest Festival

Mr Sainsbury wishes it to be known that he intends to ignore the silly petition signed by 99 percent of the parishioners, objecting to the decoration of the church with fish-flavoured marrows and 12-metre long blue carrots.

He has asked me to inform the congregation that there is no possible reason why we should not give thanks to the Lord (Sainsbury) for his bounteous gifts to the parish, made possible by the miracle of genetically-modified food products. We will, as usual, be singing the hymn

*"We plough the fields and scatter
The GM seed on the land
And if it comes up luminous
Won't that just be grand?"*

T.B.

# A WARNING TO PARISHIONERS FROM THE VICAR'S WIFE, MS CHERIE BOOTH QC

I would like to take this opportunity to warn all readers of this newsletter not to repeat the malicious slander recently put about that my life coach Ms Carole Caplin has been banned from the vicarage and her door key taken away and given back to Mr Mandelson. Ms Caplin and I are still the very best of friends and continue to enjoy our twice-weekly yoga workouts at the St Albion's Bio-energy and Holistic Pyramid Centre in Bonkers Road (the old Fire Station).

It is also not true that Carole is writing a book called *'How I Made A Fortune Out Of My Friendship With The Blairs'*. It is called *'How I Would Never Write A Book About The Blairs Like Mr Campbell'* and will contain nothing indiscreet or derogatory in any way, as per her contract agreeing that any breach of confidence might well lead to a reintroduction of the death penalty for treason and/or damages for ten billion pounds.

**C. Booth, Matrix Chambers, C/o The Vicarage.**

# Seasonal Meditation

Autumn is a sad time when all the hopes of spring and summer fade away and then decay. The leaves which were once so bright and so admired by everyone become tarnished and tired and eventually just drop off. But that is the way it must be and, fortunately, the story does not end there.

There is a new leaf waiting to take its rightful place in the vicarage, and everyone will say "Why wasn't this new leaf there all along? It's so much better than that old one!"

G.B. (The parish's 'mystery poet'!)

# Amateur Dramatic Society

Parishioners are particularly asked not to attend the latest production being staged in the Church Hall by our local thespians. Their new offering, *The Deal*, is a silly fantasy about a parish in which the vicar has agreed with the treasurer to hand over to him the running of the parish.

This totally implausible scenario is made even more unlikely by the portrayal of the vicar as a hypocritical, public-school type and the treasurer as an honest, down-to-earth Scotsman. Honestly, no wonder no one goes to the theatre any more, when this sort of thing is looked on as entertainment.

**Vicar's Rating: 0 out of 10.**

# ST ALBION PARISH NEWS

*17th October 2003*

*Hullo!*

And I know there's only been one topic of conversation around the parish this week, which modesty would normally forbid me to mention!

But I gather there are still a number of parishioners who've been unable to see the video of my talk at our recent outing to the seaside at Bournemouth (despite Mr Mandelson's much-appreciated efforts to get a cassette to every home in the parish!).

Let me remind you of why my few 'well-chosen words' went down so well with all of you who were lucky enough to be in the hall!

Firstly, I was brave enough to admit that the past few months have not been easy for your vicar!

But, secondly, I made it clear I have been sustained all along by my unshakeable faith – my faith in myself.

That's what's important, isn't it, when we are put to the test in this life – we turn to the one person we know we can always rely on. Me. (And thank you all for cheering so loudly when I admitted that to you – that really meant a lot to me, I can tell you!)

You may remember I told a little story here about someone else who'd found himself in a similar position, when some of his closest followers had tried to betray him!

And, hey, he was sorely tempted to pack it all in, and let someone take on the responsibility for a change.

And don't we all have that 'take this cup away from me' moment at some time or another in our lives? Well, I don't obviously! I stick to my guns through thick and thin, regardless of what fainthearts like Mr Cook and Mrs Short may say!

And it was at this point in my talk that I was inspired to use the metaphor that had everyone on their feet cheering and cheering until I thought it would never stop!

"I don't do reverse gear!" I said. "I just put my foot down on the motorway of life (in the third lane, of course!) and don't stop until I've reached wherever it is we're going!"

Though I say it myself, I'm not surprised that everyone was kind enough to say on the bus going home that it was the best speech by anyone they had ever heard in their whole lives, and how completely it erased the unfortunate memory of the rather embarrassing performance by our parish treasurer the previous day!

I don't in any way wish to be personal or rude about Gordon's efforts, because I know he was trying his best to be helpful!

But, honestly, all that tired old stuff about how much better things were in the old days (yawn!) may have gone down well with one or two of our very old parishioners! But, oh dear me, do we really want to go back to the old creed and all that dated language from the past, when we've spent all this time and effort bringing the parish up to date?

Could I extend my metaphor and suggest that poor old Gordon, God bless him, seems only to have one gear, and that **is** reverse!

Watch out everyone, Gordon's about to run you over! (Only joking, Gordon, no offence, but no wonder you were looking so miserable and didn't join in the clapping when Mr Mandelson was holding up his "Applaud or else!" board!)

It's always embarrassing when someone makes a fool of themselves in public, but I do think we must all try to show some compassion and stop going on about it!

Yours,

Tony

---

 ## To Remember In Your Prayers

● Our poor treasurer Mr Brown, who made such a fool of himself in public at our outing to the seaside. Let us pray that he will learn his lesson and not get ideas above his station, and that everyone else will not keep bringing it up at every opportunity! T.B.

---

## MILLENNIUM TENT UPDATE

VERY GOOD NEWS! We have had a generous offer from a highly reputable American company called the Godfather Corporation of Las Vegas who have imaginative plans to turn the tent into a casino with slot machines, roulette wheels and other fun games for the whole family. (It will be "an amazing day out" for everyone, as Mr Gerbil used to say when he ran the tent!)

There is, however, a slight problem, in that the entire board of the American company are serving a prison sentence of 99 years, so it may be a little time before we can finalise the arrangements. So, in the meantime, may I ask everyone again not to use it as a dumping ground for old PCs, microwaves and fridges. P.M.

# Service Of Thanksgiving For The Vicar's Deliverance

*T*hanks to everyone for the big turn out to our special thanksgiving service for the Vicar's deliverance from all his enemies. What a shame that this wonderful occasion should have been marred by the visiting preacher, Dr

Williams, who struck what everyone felt was a wrong note by suggesting that I was "going to be called to account".

Let's face it, there are many people who will be called to account when the time comes and perhaps it would be unfair to name them, but false preachers from Wales with beards could well be to the forefront on judgement day!! T.B.

# FIGHT THE FLAB WITH THE VICAR!

The parish is rapidly turning into a bunch of fatties!! So it's time for our portly parishioners (no offence, Mr Prescott!!) to follow the example of Cherie and myself and use the Caplin Holistic Pyramid Diet. As Carole says at our personal organic exercise sessions, "You can find your thinner self".

*Here it is – Carole's three-step recipe to losing pounds:*
1. Give the pounds to Carole
2. Er...
3. That's it.

*(Are you sure this is right?*
*Churchwarden and Acting Editor, P. Mandelson)*

**The Vicar: Going nowhere fast!!**

# ST ALBION PARISH NEWS

## *31st October 2003*

*Hullo!*

And I know there's only one thing you want to know this week – how am I?

The answer, you'll be delighted to hear, is that your vicar is absolutely fine! In fact, I've never felt better!

The doctors all say that they've never seen a healthier man admitted to Casualty with heart problems!

That's how fit I am! In fact, as one of the paramedics said as he carried me into the ambulance, "Vicar, if I was in as great shape as you are, I'd be a very happy man!"

Not that it wouldn't be a surprise if someone under as much pressure as I have been didn't have a few heart problems!

Let's face it, for the past seven years, since I took over at St Albion's, I've had just about the most gruelling workload any vicar can ever have faced.

Hey, I'm not complaining! Someone's got to do the work around here! And it's not going to be certain other people I could name, who seem to be rather too busy worrying about all their homes, or their new baby, or trying to get everyone in the parish to walk around with an ID card (and probably in braille too!).

No, I don't regret in any way that I am a 24/7 'rolling' vicar! And in case any of you have forgotten, here are just some of the things I've managed to achieve!

Firstly, I've rid the world of Satan, with the help of my good friend the Rev. Dubya, of the Church of the Latter-Day Morons.

Secondly, I have rebuilt our Mission to Northern Ireland which has been a huge success (and the fact that unfortunately it was burned down again immediately, just gives us the opportunity to rebuild it yet again, even stronger and better than before!).

As for my other achievements, they are too many to mention, such as setting new targets for ridding St Albion's of chewing gum on the pavements (not clever or funny!); sacking Mr Cook as our church organist after his disgraceful behaviour in the organ loft with Gaynor (**not** something we'll be reading about in his diaries, I expect!); and of course the huge success of our Millennium Tent project (which, in spite of my repeated requests to the contrary, is STILL being used as a receptacle for unwanted PCs, fridges, stereos and dead pets).

But enough of my achievements! I am only mentioning them at all to help you realise just what an amazing strain running this parish is, and how any normal man would be in his grave by now with the colossal pressures I have to live under, hour by hour, day by day, week by week, trying to make your parish a better and happier place to live in!

So it's hardly surprising that for a few minutes last week the medics pronounced me as technically 'dead'.

But when I saw the 'white light', I heard a heavenly voice saying "Hey, look Tony, you can't come up here yet! You've still plenty of work to do back there on earth!"

And then I woke up and, do you know, I felt 100 percent better than I have ever felt in my entire life.

So let's not have any more of this silly chatter that I am just looking for an excuse to retire, and to hand over the parish to someone else!

No way José (or indeed Gordon, for that matter!).

I'm here to stay, OK? As it says in that wonderfully inspiring old story of the hard-working Lazarus, "and, lo, he rose up from his death bed, much healthier than before. And all the world was amazed!" *(St Paul's Letter to the Doctor)*.

Yours as 'fit as a fiddle',

*Tony*

## Remembrance Sunday

This year we shall be remembering all those who nearly laid down their lives in the service of their country, but are now feeling much better, thank you very much! The Roll Call of Honour (one name) will be read out by a representative of the St Albion's Scout Troop (L. Blair).

## THANK YOU!
### From the Acting Editor Mr Mandelson

As you all know I turned 50 last week and I was extremely grateful that not a single person sought to draw attention to the fact by sending me a card or a present.

Thank you all very much and I would just like to remind you that I do know where you all live. P.M.

# Visit of Reverend Dubya

We are very pleased to announce that Rev. Dubya Bush of the Church of the Latter-Day Morons will be honouring the parish with a three day "pray-in" on November 19.

I want you to put this important date in your diaries and I hope that all of you who can will be there to give Rev. Dubya a St Albion's style welcome that he will never forget. And by that I don't mean Miss Short, Mr Cook and Mr Livingstone heading a protest parade with banners saying "Killer Bush is Satan" and other unhelpful slogans.

I plan to show the Rev. Dubya some of the good things that are happening here, such as the Millennium Tent, the cardboard model of the new foundation hospital, etc, etc.

Hope to see you there! T.B.

# EXCOMMUNICATION

At a specially convened meeting of the PCC the Vicar solemnly proclaimed that Mr George Galloway was a heretic and blasphemer who would henceforth be cast into outer darkness "for taking the name of the Vicar in vain".

*T.B. writes: Nobody must speak to him ever again*

# Coffee Morning

The Vicar's wife wishes it to be known that, on the medical advice of Ms Caplin, all parish coffee mornings have been cancelled indefinitely. On Sunday mornings, the normal coffee and biscuits after the service will be replaced by health-giving tisanes from the Caplin Collection, including ragwort, digitalis (and belladonna for our treasurer, Mr Brown!).  C.B.

# ST ALBION PARISH NEWS

*14th November 2003*

*Hullo!*

And I am sure everyone in the parish will want to join me in congratulating our treasurer Mr Brown and his good lady Sarah on the birth of their son John Smith Brown.

It's always a matter for particular rejoicing when an elderly parishioner finally manages to get married and have a child and, of course, we are all very happy for Gordon!

But isn't there a danger that an older father may get rather too carried away by the experience of fatherhood and start imagining that he is the only person who has ever had a baby?

I mean, you don't see the rest of us going on and on about nappies and sleepless nights, do you?

Or calling in the local newspaper to take endless pictures of the proud father posing with the baby in his arms?

Isn't there rather a good verse in the scriptures where one of the old prophets says "Been there, done that"?

I have to say, those wise words rang rather a bell in my mind when I saw all those pictures of Gordon grinning away like a monkey instead of putting on that usual dour, miserable expression that suits him so much better.

When Cherie and I produced our *fourth* child (before Gordon had even got round to getting married, I might add!), you didn't see me prancing about, showing off little Leo to all the world, and posing for pictures romping with him on the floor of the vicarage.

We hear a lot these days about 'post-natal depression', don't we?

But isn't there another condition just as worrying called 'post-natal elation', where a new father gets so full of himself that he begins to think that he can do anything, including other people's jobs!

I don't want to tell tales out of school, but I was a little surprised to be told that Gordon was actually demanding a place as of right on my special NEC working group (New Evangelical Convention).

This was quite embarrassing for me, because Gordon knows perfectly well that this is a committee only for people I can really trust, and that the last thing we need is anyone trying to make trouble at our meetings by challenging the general line that we've agreed amongst myself!

There's always someone at a meeting who wants to raise some point of order about something trivial, like whether we should have the collection in euros or not.

Goodness me, we could talk all night about that one, couldn't we, and still get no nearer to a decision!

Z-z-z-z-z, Gordon, on that one! As it says in the New Labour Bible, "Get real!" *(Book of Wislon, 4.16).*

So, sorry Gordon! As it says in another memorable passage from the Good Book, "Many are called, but only one is chosen" *(Revelations of St Antony The Divine, 24.2).*

And that applies, not just to some silly committee, but to the most important job of all!

So, let's all pray that in a few days' time Mr Brown will be coming down to earth, forgetting about his baby and getting back to doing the modest but useful job in the parish administration that he is being paid for!

Yours, Tony

(not forgetting little Leo!)

## The Vicar at Remembrance Sunday

*Look, it's time to forget all this and* **move** *on!*

## A Message From Rev. Dubya, the Grand Tabernacle, Salt Tears City

My fellow Righteous Brothers in Englandland!
I am greatly looking forward to my visit to your
beautiful country, wherever it is! Mrs Dubya and I
are counting the days until we can break bread with
you and take a tour of your fabled heritage sites:

- Windsor Palace
- Buckingham Castle
- the Leaning Tower of Harrods
- Shakespeare-upon-Avon

Brother Rumsfeld says he is very sorry not to be with us on this
occasion, but he and Sister Condy are having to stay home to keep
ever vigilant lest Satan creeps in in the middle of the night "seeking
whom he may devour"!

*Yours in the Lord! Rev. Dubya*

## St Albion's Welcomes Rev. Dubya!

**Mr Straw writes:**

We are all hugely looking forward to the visit which is shortly to be paid to the parish by our good friend the Rev. Dubya of the Church of the Latter-Day Morons.

I know that a tiny minority of 100,000 or so troublemakers are thinking of trying to spoil what should be a wonderful day of celebration, so let me just warn them that the long-range weather forecasters are predicting torrential rain, hurricane winds, deadly lightning and a possible collision with a 75-million-tonne asteroid! So it is my advice to any would-be troublemakers that they would be well advised to stay at home and watch the Rev. Dubya on our local TV News, driving down the High Street with the Vicar in glorious sunshine! J.S.

## BONFIRE NIGHT

There was a very good turn-out for our parish bonfire night, which was greatly enjoyed by all. This year, we advertised our display as "The Fireworks Of Mass Destruction", which meant that everyone had to stand around gazing into the sky imagining that they were looking at the most awesome fireworks show they had ever seen (complete with poison gas!).

The 'guy' was made up to look like Saddam Hussein, but unfortunately he disappeared at the last minute and, despite looking all over the parish, he couldn't be found.

Still, everyone had a marvellous time, and many thanks to Mrs Abbott for providing the homemade humbugs which were especially enjoyed by the children. Thanks Diane! T.B.

16

# ST ALBION PARISH NEWS

*28th November 2003*

*Howdy, folks!*

You'll all have guessed why I've started this newsletter like that!

Yes, we've just had the most important visitor to the parish since I took over all those years ago!

And, hey, wasn't it amazing to see the world's top evangelist, the Rev. Dubya, actually here in St Albion's!

We've all seen pictures of him and read his inspiring exhortations to rid the world of Satan and "the powers of evilitude".

But here he was amongst us in the flesh! I don't mind admitting I haven't been so excited since we had the good fortune to welcome amongst us the Rev. Jefferson Clintstone of the Church of the Seven-Day Fornicators, with his good lady Monica!

But, I can tell you, when I shook hands with the Rev. Dubya, and he said "Hi there, Tiny!" in his slow Texan drawl, my heart skipped a beat. Except, of course, it didn't really skip a beat, because I'm absolutely fine, no matter what people say, and when I said "my heart skipped a beat", I was only using it figuratively, like Our Lord when he said "Blessed are the peacemakers", a text that has often been misinterpreted by people who take it too literally. What he really meant was "Blessed are the pacemakers", because that would help people with heart problems. Not that I'm one of them obviously, as I've just told you. Anyway, I think I'm going to have to lie down for a while after all the excitement of the Rev. Dubya's visit!

So, instead of carrying on with this newsletter, I'm going to give you a real treat: the chance to read for yourselves the full text of the Rev. Dubya's awe-inspiring sermon, which unfortunately so few parishioners were able to hear, after Mr Blunkett of our Neighbourhood Watch called in 3000 heavily armed security guards to ring the church with a wall of steel, while the Rev. Dubya preached from inside a specially installed bullet-proof pulpit. (Incidentally, my apologies to all those members of the congregation who were unavoidably locked into the vestry over the weekend when the church was "sealed off" – but at least it was all in a good cause!)

*Tony*

# *That Rev. Dubya Sermon In Full*

*Brothers and sisters, here in Englandland,*
Welcome to my world. And a very special brand of welcome to your good pastor, the Rev. Toby, and his good lady Queen Elizabeth, who have made us feel so at home in their beautiful Buckingham Hotel.

I salute my brother-in-arms, Toby, who has been prepared to make any sacrifice to support me in my great crusade to rid the world for once and for all of extreminosity and the power of Satan.

Toby has not worried for a moment what people here in Englandland might think of him! Even though he has had to face the whips and scorpions of his enemies in his own congregation, he has not for one second shirked from his duty to back me in all I am trying to do.

For, as it says in the Good Book, "Woe unto ye, when all shall speak well of you. Yea, verily and indeedy-do" *(Book of Moron)*.

I have a dream, brothers and sisters. A dream of the Holy Landland changed in the twinkling of an eye. Where today there may be tyranny and cvilitude, there may tomorrow be a reign of democracy and peacitude.

Is that not a vision worth pursuing? I say unto ye, yea, verily, yea!

And will you be with me, o people of Great Britainville, the heirs, are you not, of William Wilbursmith, who saved the world from slavery?

Our two peoples have always, down the centuries, fought together, as we did in the great wars of Suez and Vietnam.

And now we must pray together that the Lord may grant us release from the burden of having to keep the peace in Iraqland (and, while he is about it, to grant also a second term to his right-hand man here on earth!).

In this prayer, I am joined by Brother Colin and Sister Condy, who are here with me today, joining their prayers to your heartfelt shouts of "Go home, warmonger", which I know in your language means "Please stay here amongst us, for you are the bringer of peace".

And now let us all sing the Battle Hymn of the Republican party, 'Mine Eyes Have Seen The Glory Of The Coming Of Myself'*.

*\*Parishioners will of course recognise this in its more familiar English version 'Gordon Brown's body lies a-mouldering in the graveyard'!! T.B.*

18

# Congratulations!

May I offer my warmest congratulations on behalf of the parish to our splendid rugby team for their glorious victory over the weekend. Before I am accused of "jumping on the band wagon" or "hijacking" their great achievement, can I make it clear that I have no desire to try and capitalise on their heroic feats. Instead I will be holding a simple low-key champagne victory parade through the streets of the parish, culminating in a grand firework display and a parish holiday to be known as "Blair Day" in honour of the team. T.B

**The vicar in his new close-fitting vestment. By local artist Mr de la Nougerede!!**

## Talking Point

You know, when one looks at the winning English rugby team one can't help thinking – yes, it's a team effort but in the end doesn't it all depend on one particularly brilliant player who can be relied upon to get it right at the important moments whilst the big, thick, so-called heavyweights lumber about behind him, giving away penalties and making the star's job even harder??! Just a thought! T.B.

 ## Parish Postbag

*Dear Son-in-law,*

*You make me sick the way you cosy up to the Reverend Dubya. Well, you can stick your rotten Britain up your*

       *Yours sincerely,*
       *Tony Booth,*
       *The Old Off-Licence,*
       *The High Street.*

The editor reserves the right to cut all letters. P.M.

## Creche News

Mrs Hodge, the parish Children's Officer, has promised to take action over the terrible problem of abuse in the parish. She tells me that she has been suffering a lot of abuse recently, with people shouting "Resign, you dreadful woman" at her in the street. This must obviously stop at once. T.B

# ST ALBION PARISH NEWS

*12th December 2003*

*Hullo!*

And I certainly don't mean "goodbye", whatever certain parishioners might be hoping!

No, as Christmas approaches, this is the time of year when we all look forward, not back! Which is why I am celebrating this Advent-tide by holding what I have called my "Big Conversation".

Those who were in church for Evensong last Sunday will remember that this comes from two Latin words "conus" (which means "to pretend") and "versatio" (which means "to listen!").

So I am asking everyone in the parish to think very hard and to tell me their real concerns about the way the parish is going.

And, I promise you, what I want to hear are the views of ordinary people.

I'm not interested in the same old gripes from the grumpy brigade whom we hear far too much of – Mr Cook, Mrs Short, Mr Dobson, Mr Kilfoyle, Mr Marshall-Andrews – gosh, I'm getting bored just listing them!

No, let's hear it for a change from the guy at the back of the church who wants to say what a great job we are doing in the parish, and how well everything is going!

We don't hear much from him, do we, which is why I want to give him the chance to join in the Conversation.

And what about the woman who wants to say "thank you" to the Rev. Dubya for his inspiring crusade against the evil Satan wherever he may be found?

Or what about the young student who wants to tell us how willing he is to pay back what he owes the community for his studies (and possibly a little more on top!)

I could talk for hours to him, couldn't you?

And then there's the little old lady who's been waiting for years for a hip operation. She might well want to tell me that she really doesn't mind at all, because she appreciates that there are plenty of more deserving cases who have every right to be treated first, even if they have to go private!

Are you beginning to get the idea? Real people, real conversations, real progress!

And the list goes on. The phone rings and there is a man who's just been burgled. What he wants to tell me is that the police have immediately caught the culprit!

Of course he can't tell me that, because the police are so busy these days, what with all these speeding offences, that they simply haven't got time to arrest burglars.

But our friend knows that, and he shows a real appreciation for everything the police are unable to do.

Hey, I'll be honest with you. I've learned a lot talking to these people, or at least I will when I do talk to them. And I think you will too!

Because, as we read somewhere in the scriptures, "yea, verily, for it is better to talk than it is to listen" (*Letter of St. Peter to the Mandelsonians, Ch.14*).

So between now and Christmas I want all of you to spend a few minutes every day thinking of all those important things which could make similar topics for our "Big Conversation".

And to inspire your letters, faxes, e-mails or texts (gosh, I'm beginning to sound like one of those phone-in programmes, aren't I?), here are the words of a chorus which we are going to try out at this week's evensong.

*Join, join, join the Conversation*
*Everybody in the nation*
*Black or white or brown or gay*
*Talking is the only way*
*Join, join, join the Conversation*
*Let me hear your information*
*Old or straight or rich or gay*
*Talking is the only way*
*Join, join, join the Conversation*
*Come to me with your frustration*
*Fat or thin or tall or gay*
*Talking is the only way*

© *Words and music T Blair 2003.*

Tony

# A THOUGHT FOR CHRISTMAS

As the season of goodwill is upon us we should perhaps give some thought to the Seven Deadly Sins:- and by far the worst of them, I think we all agree is Envy. I want to tell you a story about a man who desperately wanted his best friend's job.

Let's call him Mr Green and his best friend Mr Wonderful. Now Mr Green lived next door to Mr Wonderful and desperately "coveted" (as they used to call it in the olden days from the Latin covetus meaning greedy, ungrateful or Scottish) his house and his position.

Mr Wonderful however wisely realised that Mr Green was sick with jealousy and that this all-consuming envy was making Mr Green ill.

So he decided to tell the world that yes, Mr Green did want his job but this desire was "not ignoble".

"It is, however," he said, "an appalling sin for which there will be no forgiveness and Mr Brown should be deeply ashamed of himself." *T.B*

# THE VISIT OF MONSIGNOR CHIRAC TO THE PARISH

**The photographer asked Jacques to say "Cheese-eating-surrender-monkey"!!!! T.B**

# That St Albion Rugby Team Victory Parade Timetable In Full

11.00am    Vicar welcomes St Albion's Rugby Team onto open-top bus outside vicarage (Team inside, vicar on top)

11.20am    Bus proceeds down St Albion's High Street stopping outside Mr Dirty Desmond's Adult Entertainment Centre for photo opportunity of the Vicar accompanied by readers' wives and Asian babes

11.30am    Bus proceeds for short distance before stopping outside Mr Dirty Digger's Slags 'n' Mags Emporium for photo opportunity of the Vicar accompanied by page 3 "Rugger Stunna", Tracy Snodgrass, 17, wearing special "Jonny Wilkinson" thong

11.45am    Bus stops outside St Albion's railway station to sign autographs for commuters delayed by victory parade

12.00pm    Bus returns to vicarage for victory lunch with selected guests including friends of the vicar and no-one else

12.15pm    Drinks and nibbles to be served including Lager and Limelight, Cashin nuts and Bandwagon Wheels. No coffee in case the vicar has a heart attack

12.30pm    Vicar leads victory community singing with old favourites including "Glory, Reflected Glory Alleluia" and the legendary "Swing High Sweet Opinion Poll"

12.45pm    Rugby team depart leaving Vicar in charge of cup "for safekeeping".

# TIDINGS OF GREAT JOY

### *HALLELUJAH!*

*Ding-dong-merrily-on-high!*
*In heaven the bells are ringing!*

They certainly are today, as we celebrate the greatest Christmas present the human race has ever been given.

Not that we should be merely rejoicing just because the Great Satan has at last been captured, as was foretold by the prophets, such as Brother Rumsfeld and Sister Condy (not to mention myself!).

Obviously this is a very solemn time, when the hopes and fears of all the years are centred on an obscure little town somewhere in the Middle East.

Think about it – isn't it the Christmas story all over again? Except in reverse.

There amid the palm trees is the humble dwelling where, in the darkness, the Prince of Evil is at last to be revealed to the world.

Yet to this lowly place of poverty came visitors from afar, only too eager to see for themselves the devil in human form.

But who were the Three Wise Men, you ask? Can the children think of anyone?

I'll give you a clue. Two of them have names which begin with "B"!

That's right, young Asif – the Rev. Bush, the Rev. Blair, and the Spanish one whose name we can't remember!

Anyway, they journeyed long and they journeyed far, guided only by the light of the Lone Star of Texas shining in the sky above them!

They didn't waver in their search! They didn't falter in their quest! They didn't listen when the doubters said "You'll never find him"!

This isn't a day to crow over those sadly misguided doubters, because people like Mr Cook, Mrs Short, Mr Kilfoyle, Mr

Galloway and Mr Marshall-Andrews will be feeling silly enough today, without me having to name them!

So it would be in the spirit of Christmas not to mention them at all!

And what's the message of this wonderful Christmas story?

It is that when something truly miraculous and profoundly significant happens, everything else in our lives looks trivial and unimportant.

All those things which normally fill our minds and get people so worked up suddenly fall away in the light of the greater truth!

I bring "tidings of great joy"! That's the message! Truly it is the "Good News" we've all been waiting for (and remember it was not the Rev. Dubya who announced it first but your own vicar, right here in St Albion's!).

And, compared with that world-shattering event, who any longer is the slightest bit interested in "weapons of mass destruction" or poor Dr Kelly (who thought he was Walter Mitty!), let alone poor old Mr Hutton, still "burning the midnight oil" to produce his report that no one is going to read!

He might as well pack up and go home and enjoy his Christmas turkey like everyone else!

Never mind, Mr Hutton – I'm sure the whole parish is grateful to you for all the time you have put in, which, sadly, now turns out to have been wasted.

So this year I can wish you all a very happy and joyful Christmas indeed – the happiest I can remember for many years!

Yours in exaltation,

Tony

## New at St Albion's!!!

There will be some specially-adapted carols at this year's service of Midnight Mass Destruction, including:

"Saddam Lay Y-Bounden" (*Choir only*)

"Little Donkey (Carry Saddam Safely to the Gaol)" (*Children*)

"God Arrest Ye Bearded Gentlemen" (*All*)

*Words and music adapted by T. Blair*

# Yuletiditudal Message From Rev. Dubya of the Church of the Latter-Day Morons

*SEASONAL GREETINGS* to my brethren in Englandia! And my fraternital regards to your brave pastor Tony Bear and his lovely wife Cherylene for standing by me when the clock struck noon!

WE GOT HIM!!!

That's the message. Dead-Eye Satan has been cornered in his lair, trapped like a skunk in a bunker! And the lily-livered rat wouldn't even go for his gun!! That's the kinda of no-good low-down rattlesnake Satan is! A yellow-bellied coyote if ever there was one!

And what do we do now, sheriff? you ask. Don't you guys watch any westerns? We take him from the gaol and we hang him high! Glory allelulia! Amen! Now I know some of you backsliders in GreatBritainland want to see the county judge ride over and give Dead-Eye Satan a fair trial!

Fine by me! As long as we string him up afterwards!

Then it's back to the sheriff's office for a damn good cup of coffee and one of Laura's googleberry muffins!

Yessirree!

A Happy Xmastide to you all!!

Rev. Dubya, U.S. Marshall

# PARISH PANTO UPDATE

nd a huge welcome to our old friend Mr Livingstone from the Aquatic Pet Centre (Newts 'r' Us in the High Street) who has very kindly agreed to come back to star in this year's panto as the Lord Mayor of London! Despite our differences in the past (Ken could never keep to the script!), we are all delighted that such a popular local figure has agreed to let bygones be bygones (as has the vicar!!!), so that we can all produce the best possible show for the mums and dads and boys and girls!

Here's just a sneak preview of this year's hilarious script, adapted from one of the best-loved of all panto tales.

## Act One: On a high road to London

*The vicar has asked Dick Livingstone, a poor newt-lover, to rally to the cause.*

**Vicar:** Hey, Dick, turn again! I'm always turning, even though I've got no reverse gear!

**Ken:** You look lovely in your reverse gear! You'll be winning the Turner Prize next!

**Vicar:** Do you really promise that you've turned over a new leaf, Ken?

**Ken:** Oh yes I have!

**Audience:** Oh no you haven't!

**Ken:** Oh yes I have!

**Audience:** Watch out vicar, he's behind you!

**Ken:** Oh no I'm not!

## Act Two: The City Hall

*Enter desperate crowd of citizens.*

**Citizens:** Your Worship, we are being overrun by a dreadful plague of pigeons!

**Mayor Ken:** Fear not, I have a cunning plan! All pigeons will be charged £5 to enter the congestion zone. That should sort them out!

**Audience:** Oh no it won't!

**Ken:** In that case I'll have to send my cat, Red Kat, to kill them all.

**Red Kat:** Mao-mao.

## Act Three: The Hustings

*A sign reads "Grand Tourney – Ye Dick Livingstone Battles Ye Tory Squire, Shagger Norris (sponsored by Jarvis)".*

**Vicar:** We don't want to give the game away by letting you know who wins, do we?

**Audience:** Oh yes we do!

**Vicar:** Alright then, the winner is me! Thanks for your help, Ken!

## DON'T FORGET – BOOK EARLY – BECAUSE THIS PROMISES TO BE THE BEST PANTO EVER!!!!

# ST ALBION PARISH NEWS

*9th January 2004*

*Hullo!*

And a very Happy New Year to all parishioners!

Ring out the old, ring in the new! That's what we usually say isn't it? But, hey, before you pull on those bell ropes, let's look at it a different way, shall we?

Instead of looking forward and making a lot of silly promises that we can't keep, let's look back at all the promises that we made in 2003 and that some of us *did* keep!

● Satan has been o'erthrown! (Promise kept!)

● Peace has been brought to the ancient lands of the Middle East! (Promise kept!)

● Those weapons of mass destruction have been found! (Promise kept, again!)*

I could go on all night. But I don't want to sound like one who "bloweth his own trumpet"! *(Book of Satchmo 7.3)*

So, **I'm** very happy to look back on a real "year of achievement"!

But I know there are some people who won't be so keen to look back on the past year.

Our treasurer Mr Brown, for example, with that embarrassing speech he made at the parish outing to the seaside!

Honestly, the bit where he suggested that he could do my job better than me was toe-curling, wasn't it?

The less said about it the better! But wasn't it terrible? And the fact that hardly anyone clapped, compared to the response when I made my own speech the next day, must have made him feel really foolish!

You know when you have a dream that you're standing up on a stage somewhere, in front of a whole crowd of people, and you suddenly realise that you haven't got any trousers on? That's how it must have been for poor Mr Brown, except that it was for real!

And talking about people with no trousers on, what about our former organist, Mr Cook? He resigned from the PCC on what he rather grandly called "a point of principle"!

And how embarrassed he must have felt when the Great Satan was finally tracked down, hiding away in a dirty hole in the ground, with a beard almost as silly and unnecessary as Mr Cook's own!

Yes, he's another one who won't be wanting a 'replay' of 2003 in a hurry!

And what about poor Mrs Short? I expect, with her sad history of alcoholism and mental instability, she'll be looking for some pretty expert counselling to help her when she looks back on a year of failure and treason!

She called me "reckless"! If I were very unkind, I might even reply "better than being legless, Clare"! (But I won't because it's not my style!)

And talking of leglessness, I think we should all spare a thought this New Year for our former parish solicitor Mr Lairg!

There's yet another person in the parish who may wish to avert his gaze from what happened in the past 12 months (as he sits there clutching a glass of whisky with Mrs Dewar!).

And those are just some of the more prominent parishioners who've got a lot to forget as they look back on 2003!

But I'm not forgetting all those ordinary members of the congregation who took it upon themselves to march up and down the parish, holding up the traffic and shouting rude remarks about our good friend the Rev. Dubya of the Church of the Latter-Day Morons!

Rather a lot of you, weren't there? And I expect you're all feeling suitably contrite, now that what our friend the Rev. Dubya calls "evilitude" has been utterly cast down, and those "weapons" have been well and truly found, as I always prophesied!*

But the one I feel really sorry for is poor Mr Hutton who, despite everything that has happened, still seems determined to go on writing his laborious report on all sorts of things which, frankly, no one is interested in any more!

It is obviously very commendable that Mr Hutton feels obliged to carry on scribbling away at the report that I asked him to write, but he must now be looking back at the year and wondering why he wasted so much of his and everybody else's time!

So, when it comes to our first evensong of the New Year, let's join together in a special chorus I have written to celebrate the old year:

*Ring in the old, ring out the new*
*That's the message for me and for you*
*Ring out the new, ring in the old*
*That's the message, so I'm told!*

And a 'Happy Old Year' to all my readers!

Tony

*Exact details to follow at a future date. T.B.

# Kidz Korner

★ I wonder how many of the children will recognise the latest star of the popular American TV series The Simpsons. Yes, it's your very own vicar – being watched by millions of people all over the world!

I don't mind admitting I was pretty excited to be asked to appear in the world's favourite TV show (and in my view, the best!). I know that some of the older members of the congregation may not have thought it was very dignified for their vicar to be confused "on the screen" with Mr Bean, who is an idiot who can never get anything right!

But of course it was only a joke! They knew perfectly well who I really was! And, anyway, Mr Bean is the most famous British person in America, where he is not looked on as funny at all!

Enjoy the rest of your holiday, kids, and don't watch too much telly!

Your vicar, *Tony*

## COLOURING COMPETITION

★ Here is a picture of Mr Brown making his speech at our seaside outing. Colour his face with an appropriate crayon.

Suggestions:
> Red for embarrassment
> Green for envy
> Blue for depression
> White for shock
> Yellow for cowardice
> Black for anger, etc

*Send your drawings to Mr Brown, c/o The PCC! The winner will get a free outing to the Millennium Tent Winter Experience, where they can have a magical tour of the old fridges and burnt-out Volvos that have become such an attraction in the parish.*

*23rd January 2004*

*Hullo!*

Of course there's been only one talking point in the parish in recent days, and that was my guest-appearance as a top DJ on our local hospital radio's most popular morning show "Good Morning Bedblockers!"

For those of you who missed it, my performance was so enjoyed by everyone who heard it that I know some of you would like to be able to read the highlights of the programme in "print form"!

So here it is.

## THE 'GOOD MORNING BEDBLOCKERS' SHOW

VICAR: Hi everyone! It's Tony here, your vicar, taking over for the next two hours here on Radio St Albion's FM93.86... have I got that right, Steve?... ha, ha, ha... so here goes, give us a call on 0202 0202, and you can ask me absolutely anything you like, so long as it's been cleared beforehand! I'm sure you'll all agree that's fair?

So let's go to our first caller, Daniel from Tesco Road.

CALLER: Good morning, Vicar, how are you?

VICAR: I'm very well, thanks! Next caller.

CALLER: No, no, that wasn't my question! My question is, why do so many people in the parish seem to want you to quit – because of your views on the war and the students and pretty well everything?

VICAR: Well, Daniel, that's a very good point, and certainly something I'm prepared to think about and take another look at. Next caller.

CALLER: It's Sandra from Asda Drive. Vicar, what I want to know is, is it true it was you who told everyone about our local GP Dr Kelly?

VICAR: Well, thanks Sandra, that's a very good question and you deserve an answer, which I'm sure Mr Hutton will be only to pleased to give you in due course. But until then, obviously, it's not for me to comment. OK?

And now it's time for the latest traffic news. Is that right Steve? Is that what I do now?

MUFFLED VOICE: Yes, get on with it, Vicar. I told you we shouldn't have had him on!

VICAR: Well, I'm afraid there's a bit of a tailback building up on the Somerfields Roundabout, stretching right back to the Texaco turn-off, which means that most of the parish is gridlocked, except for the toll road, which is closed! And I'm afraid the news about the trains is not too good either, since they've all been cancelled, as have the buses. Is that alright? And now our next caller is Peter from the Handy Mandy Agency.

CALLER: Hi Vicar, I'm a caller not a quitter! Ha, ha, ha!

VICAR: Ha, ha, ha! And now, with the time coming up to 12.00, it's time for me, your vicar, to hand back to the guy who really knows what he's doing – not that I don't! – Dave Durkin. All yours, Dave. How did I do?

DAVE: Don't give up the day job, Vicar, although a lot of people obviously want you to, ha, ha, ha!

Pretty impressive, I'm sure you'll all agree! Not my opinion, obviously, but that of an impartial observer, Treasurer Mr Brown, who said after the show that I was almost as good as Alan Partridge!

Pretty high praise, I'm sure you'll agree!

And it's only two weeks since I was compared to Mr Bean on the famous Simpsons show!

I'd better be careful, or I might get big-headed, which I wouldn't obviously, because I'm not that sort of guy!

**_DJ Tony 'Tony Blackburn' Blair!_**

# *Theology for Modern Man –*
# *Our Beliefs Explained*

## No 94: Totality

*A* number of you have noticed that I have recently taken to using this word "totality" in my sermons, and have asked me to explain its full doctrinal significance.

The word comes from the Greek "totus" meaning "everything", and "litus" meaning "meaning". So, basically, we can define the word as "the entire meaning" of something.

For example, if someone says "I had nothing to do with giving out Dr Kelly's name" and then says "it was me who gave out Dr Kelly's name", it would be wrong to look at either of those statements in isolation.

We have to look at both the statements together. In other words, in their totality!

Does that make sense? I know this is difficult for the children (and it's pretty difficult for some of us grown-ups as well!).

But that doesn't mean that we shouldn't try to understand these great mysteries which are so important to keeping our faith alive!

In the wonderful words of St. Peter to the Mandelsonians, "There remain these three things, brethren: faith, hope and totality. And the greatest of these is totality". T.B.

 Parish Postbag

*Dear Sir,*

*Although we may have had our differences in the past, I would like to put on record that I now consider Mr Gordon Brown to be an outstanding member of the PCC, well capable of taking over from the present*

> *Yours sincerely,*
> *Robin Cook,*
> *The Old Organ Loft,*
> *The High Street.*

The editor regrets that letters from bitter, disloyal, self-seeking adulterers may have to be cut for reasons of space. P.M.

## 𝔍𝔲𝔡𝔤𝔢𝔪𝔢𝔫𝔱 𝔇𝔞𝔶

*(Aka the day Mr Hutton delivers his report)*

A lot of people are very worried by what is being called the "Day of Judgement" (next Tuesday). All I can say to them is to quote the old text, "The innocent man who has done nothing wrong has nothing to fear. Whereas his friend Geoff Hoon is almost certainly going to get the chop" *(Book of Saving Job, 17.3)*.

# A Message from the Rev. Dubya, of the Church of the Latter-Day Morons

To my brothers and sisters, in Great Britainland, and my good friend Tony Blix and his delightful wife Cherie-Pie.

I want you all, my brothers, to journey with me on my crusade into the heavens, where a new axis of evil has been set up on the planet Mars.

This has been known as the "Red Planet" because it has been inhabited by commie terrorists, who plan to take over the entire universe, under the inspiration of their evil leader Osama bin Vader.

Unless we seek out this new Prince of Evilitude lurking in his cave on Mars, like a rattlesnake in his hole, then I can assure you, my friends, it cannot be long before he launches his so-called Weapons of Mars Destruction.

And evidence we have gleaned from a close study of the film *They*

*came From Outer Space* (b/w, 1952, Channel 5, 3.45am, Wed) proves beyond peradventure that Darth Laden is now capable of launching his UFOs within no less than 45 million light years from now!

Join with me in this great mission to find oil on Mars!

*God Bless you all,*

The Rev. George Skywalker, Jedi Knight and U.S. Marshall.

## THE PARABLE OF THE JOB HALF-DONE

There was once a man who started on a long journey and when he was halfway there, people asked him "St Anthony, why haven't you finished your journey?" To which the saint replied, "Hey, I'm only halfway there. It would be pretty silly to give up now. Especially when there are so many things to finish that I haven't even started yet."

Are you one of those silly people who might have asked St. Anthony to stop halfway? Think about it. T.B.

# ST ALBION PARISH NEWS

*6th February 2004*

# VICAR INNOCENT
# – IT'S OFFICIAL!!!

Yes, I know what some of you will be thinking! Your vicar doesn't usually start the newsletter with a great big headline, such as you might read in an ordinary newspaper!

But what else could I do? This has been the most momentous and joyous week for the parish since I first "came among you" in 1997!

For months and months, the parish has been awash with all sorts of wild rumours, malicious tittle-tattle and hurtful innuendos – not just aimed at me but at several other devoted members of the PCC and loyal servants of the parish, such as Mr Hoon and Mr Campbell.

I have been enormously proud of the courageous way in which they have stood up to this relentless and spiteful campaign without flinching, even if it unfortunately led Mr Campbell to have a nervous breakdown and to have to give up his job.

But here again there is some good news! The doctors are so pleased with his progress that he has once again been allowed out into the community, and has been popping into the vicarage to 'help out' on a part-time basis on Tuesday afternoons!

I think the first lesson that we can all take from the events of recent days is that some of us in this parish are now owed a MASSIVE APOLOGY from all those who have accused us of twisting the truth about the events which led last summer to the unfortunate death of our local GP Dr Mitty.

What has now been demonstrated for all the world to see is that the only real lie was that I and Mr Campbell had been telling lies!

So who are the people who should be first in the queue outside the vicarage to offer their apologies?

As you know, your vicar is not in the business of naming names, but at this historic moment, when the last thing I would wish to do is to crow over all those who have been proved so utterly and totally wrong, I think that if anyone put to me a number of questions about the identity of these people, I would be willing to confirm that the guilty parties who must apologise are as follows:

- Mrs Short
- Mr Cook
- Mr Marshall-Andrews
- the late Mr Dalyell
- the 108 members of the congregation who signed a petition suggesting that I should be defrocked as a war criminal
- Mr Brown
- the other Mr Brown
- all the millions of parishioners who blocked Tesco Road with banners

# THE ASSUMPTION OF INNOCENCE

The vicar was very happy with the new altarpiece

carrying such childish and wounding slogans as 'Tony BLIAR'. I would remind them that they have been captured on CCTV and that Mr Campbell has already begun the task of matching "names to faces" as part of his therapy

- everybody who works for our local media, from the chairman of the BBC's Radio Albion to the man on the corner of the High Street who hands out copies of the St Albion's Metro free sheet.

But above all, I am owed an apology by Mr Howard, the lawyer who has recently moved into the parish from Romania and who for some reason seems determined to make trouble for me with his endless nitpicking complaints about the way the parish is being run.

All I can say to all these people is that I am still waiting for them to come up with the 'Big A'!

That's 'A' for 'Abject Apology', by the way! And what they should remember is that saying sorry might be hard, as we remember from the wise words of those holy men of yore, St Simon and St Garfunkel. But, you know something? We'll all feel much better when we get it off our chests (except me, obviously, because I'm the only one who's got nothing to apologise for!).

So, to help you, Mr Mandelson has prepared an 'Apology Slip' for everyone in the parish to send in, to show how ashamed they are at having doubted the vicar's word!

---

## APOLOGY SLIP

**I would like to apologise to the vicar, humbly confessing my manifold sins and wickednesses and earnestly begging his forgiveness, which I do not deserve.**

**NAME**.........................................................................

*(No need for the address because I know where you live. PM)*

---

I have also composed a compulsory chorus for use at next Sunday's 'Evensong of Celebration', as follows:

*We're so sorry, Tony,*
   *We were in the wrong.*
*You were right as always,*
      *As you have been all along!*

(To be sung three times before the General Confession)

   Yours in glory!

   Tony

---

# *A Thanksgiving Prayer*
## *From the vicar's wife*

*Dear Lord (Hutton)*
   *We give you thanks for our salvation and for our deliverance from sleepless nights of suffering and anxiety. Yes Lord (Hutton), you heard our cry for help and in our hour of need you took mercy on us and our little children. Thank you Lord (Hutton) that we can now slumber safely in our beds knowing that you have absolved us of all our sins, not that we committed any.*
                  *Amen*

                     © *Cherie Blair, 2004.*

# FROM MR CAMPBELL
## by Email

F****** GREAT! RESULT! WE F***** THE BEEB! WE F***** GILLIGAN! WE F***** KELLY! WE F***** EVERYONE! So listen in, you scumbags, my personal integrity, my truthfulness and my 100 percent reliability on all issues is totally vindi-f******-cated! Got that, you bastards?

And anyone who disagrees better watch themselves in the dark alley behind the chip shop! I want an apology from everyone in the parish, including the vicar who forced me to step down as editor of the newsletter when it looked like that geek Hutton was not going to play ball and do what he was told!

On a happier note, there are plenty of tickets still available for my one-man show 'ALI CAMPBELL LIE ON STAGE' *(Surely 'Live'? T.B.)*. Then you can find out the real truth, when I prove for once and for all that I am not a f****** lunatic by reading every single f****** word of Mr Hutton's wonderful report, something that has never been done on stage ever before and which will last for approximately 72 hours, with one interval! Don't miss it!  A.C.

# *Apology*

*When we said in a number of recent issues of this newsletter that Mr Hutton was a bumbling old fool who was wasting his time interviewing people in the church hall about the death of Dr Mitty, and that when his absurd report finally saw the light of day it would not be worth the paper it was written on, we now realise that Mr Hutton has performed an invaluable service to the parish by producing an extraordinarily fair, balanced and fearless report. We apologise for any confusion which may unwittingly have arisen over this matter.*

*Signed Dave Hill*
*(Acting Editor, until Mr Campbell returns after his nervous breakdown)*

# ST ALBION PARISH NEWS

*21st February 2004*

## A WARNING TO ALL PARISHIONERS FROM THE FORMER CHURCHWARDEN MR MANDELSON

I have asked to be allowed a little space in this week's newsletter to spell out a few home truths to all those members of our congregation who may be on the verge of doing something very silly.

These people are still going on about Mr Hutton as if there were still any questions to be answered.

Let's get it clear in our heads, shall we? Mr Hutton explained in a way that anyone should have been able to understand, that the Vicar, Mr Campbell and Mr Hoon were absolutely and entirely free of any blame for what happened to Dr Mitty, or indeed anything else.

And if you don't believe Mr Hutton, then just you wait until the next report from Mr Butler comes out!

But I'm getting ahead of myself. What is important now is to remember what could only too easily happen to the parish, if the trouble-makers and peddlers of tittle-tattle carry on undermining the best vicar that this parish has ever had!

Do I have to spell it out? OK, I will!

In less than 45 minutes we could see everything we have worked for over the last seven years left in ruins. All it would take is our vicar, my friend Tony, to wake up one morning and say, "Hey, I've had enough!".

I can almost hear him saying, "Peter, the sheer level of ingratitude shown by this parish has finally got to me. You're the only one who's ever shown me any loyalty! Peter, you are my rock! You're a fighter, not a quitter!"

And who could blame the Vicar for having these thoughts?

How many times did I think about quitting, before deciding not to and being given the sack (twice!).

And have any of you thought what the alternative will be, if Tony decides to "take up his bed and walk"?

Some people seem to think it'll all be fine if Mr Brown, our treasurer, takes over the running of the parish during the inter regnum. Let me tell you, I've had quite a few dealings with our treasurer in recent years, and time and again I have had to warn the vicar that he is a Judas in our midst!

As for Mr Campbell, he used to go around telling people that I was too friendly with my friends the Hinduja brothers – Gotricha and Bakhanda – when I'd never met them (except once or twice), and, if you don't believe me, I suggest you dig out an old copy of Mr Hammond's wonderful report, which was every bit as conclusive as Mr Hutton's and indeed as Mr Butler's will be!

Where was I? Oh yes, Mr Campbell. Obviously, in the light of his very sad nervous breakdown, and his chronic depression at being unemployed, I have no wish to point out what a disastrous embarrassment he has been to Tony, and I am sure we all wish him the very best in his new career trying to be funny on the stage (apparently there are still quite a few tickets available!).

But this is missing the real point of why I have asked to be able to make this statement to you all!

The enemies of the parish are massing, both within and without!

All these dark forces need is for certain parishioners to turn on Tony in the way they have been doing – Mr Cook and Mrs Short will know very well whom I'm talking about – and all our achievements under Tony's inspired leadership will be blown away and forgotten. Even I myself could find myself out of work! (Not that that is why I am writing this warning to you all!) I am only thinking of Tony and of you! To try to stop you all making the most catastrophic error of your lives!

So that is why I am giving you all this last chance to come to your senses, and give Tony the support he deserves!

If you don't, you have only yourselves to blame if I have to take more drastic measures!

Remember, all your names and addresses are in my database!

Do I have to spell it out further?

Alright, I will. I know where you live!

Your **Peter "Rock" Mandelson**

*Former Churchwarden and now acting, unofficial consultant to the Vicar.*

# *Have A Great Tripoli!!!*

*Dear everyone,*
*Cherie and I are having a short break with our new friend Col Gaddafi out here in Libya! As you all know, he is a penitent who has asked for forgiveness for all his former sins, and it has been a great honour for me to be the one chosen to hear his confession and grant him absolution. Mr Mandelson has very kindly volunteered to put together the newsletter while I am away. I have no idea what he will be putting in, but I am sure he will do a great job!*
*Best wishes,* Tony

## *A Message from the Rev. Dubya, of the Church of the Latter-Day Morons*

Brothers and sisters in Great Englandland, it grieves me most grieviously to tell you that your pastor and my former friend Tony Blair has betrayed me by telling me falsitudes and untruthisms.

According to your Reverend Blair, the evil one Sattan Hussein was armed with deadly weapons that could bring anihilationness and destructitude to the whole world.

I believed him but now I find that the Reverend's words were empty. He was a false prophet that led Brother Rumsfeld, Sister Neo-Condoleezza and even myself astray – yeah, into the wilderness of erroneousness and wrongfullness. Wherefore I say, woe unto ye, Pastor Blair, who brought the world to the eve of Armageddon. Ye have borne false witness and shall be cast out into utter darkness with your chippy wife Lady Cherylene! It was all your fault!

Thus saith Dubya, holder of the great Seal of the Lord.

*(Do we still have to put this stuff in? P.M.)*

41

# Parish Scenes

The vicar is in full flow but some annoying parishioners* never know when not to ask questions!! As seen by local artist Mr de la Nougerede

*A reference to our new parishioner from Transylvania, I think! T.B.

---

## VERY IMPORTANT ANNOUNCEMENT

A lot of parishioners may have wondered what Mr Birt has been doing up there in the attic of the vicarage in the past few years. I can now reveal that he has not been just looking out of the window hoping to see some "blue sky", as some parishioners have suggested! No, John has been carrying out a "Total Audit", reviewing every single aspect of life in the parish, and he has now come up with a formula which will in future be applied to all policy decisions that we have to take!

As John himself puts it, "My Strategic Policy Equation is scientific, comprehensive and pro-active in equal measure. It provides an answer to all the known questions of the universe. It is the work of a genius, and will be known in future as 'Birt's Law'".

This is the formula. If 'D' is the desired objective, 'E' is the eventual outcome, 'S' is the steps necessary to get from 'D' to 'E', 'W' is the middle name of the US President, 'M' is Mr Mandelson, then $W+M+D = O$. (I think I've got this right!)

I will be posting more details on the vicarage website within a few days, including how this equation can be easily adapted to evaluate and resolve any problem, from the "restructuring of the flower rota" to "the re-engineering of biscuit provision at our post-service coffee sessions". T.B!

# ST ALBION PARISH NEWS

### 5th March 2004

*Hullo!*

And the "good news" this week, contrary to what you may have been hearing around the parish, is that I'm back, I'm fighting fit and, in the words of the Blessed St Margaret, Our Lady of the Handbag, "I'm glad to be going on and on and on"!

Isn't that a suitably joyous message for this time of Lent? When so many people are "giving up", I for one am not!

Can I quote you another comforting passage from the Good Book? "I will be with you always" (*Book of Job for Life*)

Isn't that reassuring to know – that whatever else may change in this fast-changing world, your vicar has every intention of remaining a pillar of strength, with no reverse gear!

And I'm glad to say that this message is beginning to get through to our parish team, even to my good friend Mr Brown, our treasurer!

In recent days Gordon has been very friendly and co-operative (not that he hadn't been before!) and several times he has called in at the vicarage to ask to borrow some sugar, because, as he explained, his projections of sugar consumption in the Brown household have proved to be based on a flawed predictive model, leaving him with a considerable shortfall in the supply-demand equation for his cup of tea! (Poor old Gordon, will he ever get anything right? Just my little joke!)

And, hey, let's get one thing straight right now. Whatever you may have heard, I'm well enough and tough enough to take the knocks. They come with the territory – the bigger the vicar, the bigger the knockers! Which brings me to Mrs Short! (No offence, Clare!) What can I say?

I'm afraid our church has a long history of over-zealous women (many of a certain age!) who claim to have seen things they haven't (documents, etc) and to have heard voices when they couldn't possibly have done so!

In medieval times, as you know, these women were called witches and were publicly burnt. Nowadays we don't do this any more, but who is to say that our solutions are any better than those of our ancestors?!

Perhaps next November 5th we could come up with someone to put on the fire who would be more relevant to the times we live in.

Let's forget poor old Guy Fawkes and burn Mrs Short instead. I'm sure we could find some old clothes from the Oxfam Shop to make it look like Clare and then use a big red balloon for her face. (No offence again, Clare!)

Let me explain – there are certain things that go on in the running of the parish that HAVE to remain confidential. Everybody knows that and Clare knows that or used to before she had her sad breakdown. So, obviously, I cannot answer her latest charges about eavesdropping and peeping toms in the PCC. As a vicar, I have taken a vow of silence on all these security matters and I will not break it, not for anyone. And I know that you wouldn't want me to. If I started to speak I know you would stop me, shouting "Vicar, don't! You are bound by your vow!" As it says in the *Book of Espion*, "There is a time to keep silent and there is a time to keep even more silent" *(13.7)*.

**The church with the vicar's new satellite listening dish! By local artist Mr de la Nougerede**

So let's not go on about Mrs Short and her problems because it would be wrong to bring up the fact that I had to sack Mrs Short from the PCC when she resigned last year, after I had done my best to persuade her to stay on by telling her that she was indispensible!

Anyway, for those of you who are worried about what has happened to poor Mrs Short recently, I'm afraid she was forced to fall back on a job as a part-time teacher in a local secondary school, recently renamed the Colonel Gaddafi Technology College (formerly the Robert Mugabe Comprehensive).

And Mrs Short didn't do too well, by all accounts! And I'm sure you will all have heard about how she couldn't keep order, arrived late and bad-tempered in the mornings and blamed her "Shortcomings" (sorry Clare, couldn't resist it!) on "problems with her hairdryer"!

Some unkind colleagues thought she looked as though she might have been drinking, reminding them of Mrs Mowlam!

It would be quite wrong for me to comment on this sort of malicious speculation! But if you asked me "Vicar, hand on heart, do you think Clare's been at the bottle?", I'd have to say "Hey, yes, it looks like it, doesn't it?" The lack of judgement, the general incompetence, the suggestions that I should resign – it all adds up, doesn't it?

Still, as I said, I don't want to go on about Mrs Short! I certainly don't have the space to make any comment on the similarity between her behaviour and that of Judas Iscariot, who received "thirty pieces of silver" as an "advance" for his book betraying his leader!

On the same theme, I don't have any space to talk about Mr Cook (who has a beard like Judas Iscariot!) who is also writing a book about me. I gather some people are saying that he needs the money to pay off his racing debts, since he has become a compulsive gambler, with a tendency to back horses which have no chance of winning (e.g. "Gay Gordon" at 500-1 in the St Albion's Handicap!).

Anyway, that's quite enough of things I haven't got space for!

All that really matters is that I am very much still here, and will remain yours for ever and ever,

Amen!

Tony

# Kiddiez Korner!

Mums, have your kids had their MMR jab yet? Don't delay or you could find yourself being arrested! Don't pay any attention to our crazy local GP Dr Wakefield, who is now totally discredited and has been found to be in the pay of several local parents with ill children.

Cherie Booth QC writes: *Can people stop asking whether Baby Leo has had the MMR jab. It's nobody's business what jabs a baby does or does not have in the privacy of the vicarage, and I warn anyone who continues to ask this question that they will be deemed to be in breach of Article 51 of the Human Rights Act which guarantees the right to privacy of all famous people and their children, on pain of extradition to Mr Blunkett's new Legal Holding Centre in Tanzania.*

 Parish Postbag

*Dear Sir,*

*I am getting more and more worried about the vicar's health. Frankly, he looks terrible, tired and old. May I suggest that he has a face-lift and he will soon find*

*Yours sincerely,*
*Sir Clifford Richard,*
*Sandy Shore, Barbados.*
*(via e-mail)*

The Editor reserves the right to cut all letters thinking that the vicar is at the point of death even when they are from such a distinguished parishioner as Sir Clifford of Richard, Knight Bachelor Boy and Living Doll (surely legend?). D.H.

## ★ HOT ★ TICKETS!!!

Mr Campbell's touring one-man show (or 'one man in the audience show', as unkind critics have been calling it!) has had its name changed from 'An Evening with Alastair Campbell' to 'An Evening with Ross Kemp from TV's EastEnders'.

Don't miss this new 'sexed-up' version of the show everybody's talking about not going to see!

All tickets still available! (Buy one, get 50 free!) P.M.

# ST ALBION PARISH NEWS

*19th March 2004*

*Hullo!*

And no, Mrs Caplin does not choose the colour of my underpants, thank you very much! Honestly, I don't know what's happening to this parish these days!

Everybody knows that Mr Foster, who started this latest silly rumour, is a liar! He lies about everything! For instance, he said that he had bought the flats for Cherie and me!

What a total lie! We bought the flats, all he did was to find them and agree the price! How can you trust a man who goes round making up those sorts of stories!

Anyone can see as soon as they set eyes on him that you can't trust a word he utters! You only have to meet him (which incidentally I have never done) to know that he is not a man who you would trust to buy a flat (let alone two!).

Let's not mince words. Mr Foster is nothing but a cheap confidence trickster, who Mr Blunkett of the Neighbourhood Watch was quite right to have expelled from the parish as an undesirable alien.

Poor Mrs Caplin is Cherie's friend, not mine, I would like to emphasise – though I have occasionally phoned her late at night in her official capacity as Underwear Colour Consultant to the Vicarage.

So, naturally, I was very sad on her behalf when Mr Foster was shown up to be nothing but a vindictive fraudster and a compulsive fantasist, who could not distinguish fact from fiction.

Imagine if a man like that was in charge of the parish! Goodness me!

He might get up in the pulpit on Sundays and tell everyone about huge weapons he'd seen in the desert, which to everybody else were completely invisible.

Or he might make the congregation's blood curdle by prophesying that we were all going to be annihilated in 45 minutes!

Someone like that wouldn't last very long, would he?

The parishioners would soon see through him, and be clamouring for someone else to take over!

So for goodness' sake, let's forget about Mr Foster, shall we, and concentrate on the things that really matter.

But before we do, can I just nail the lie once and for all that there has ever been anything "funny" about my relationship with Mrs Caplin, just because we once went through an Aztec rebirthing ceremony on the shores of Lake Poptartcatepetl, where I was transformed into the Feathered Serpent Quetzalcoatl and she became the man-devouring Alligator Goddess Titzouta.

What could be more innocent and spiritual than that?

Honestly, anyone would think there was nothing else going on in the parish except this tittle-tattle about me and Mrs Caplin!

Yours in the name of truth,

Tony

# Kidz Korner

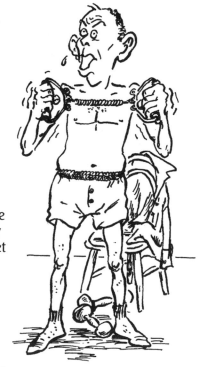

Colour in the Vicar's underpants with the colour you think would be most appropriate to his position as leader of the parish.

● Tory Blue,

● Cherie Red,

● Gordon Brown (not this one, obviously!),

● Conrad Black (nor this one!).

The winner will get a free ticket to Mr Campbell's new show. The runner-up will get TWO tickets.

**Warning:
Mr Campbell's show is
NOT suitable for children
and may contain nuts.**

# CHURCH HALL

As expected, there was a full house for the very successful *'An Evening With Mr Campbell'*, featuring the former editor of this newsletter Mr Campbell and his friend Mr Kemp (who may be familiar to some of you from his performance as the villainous murderer Bill Sykes in the St Albion's Operatic Society's recently highly-acclaimed production of Oliver)!

Mr Campbell began by telling some very amusing stories about his favourite football club (which, as some of you will know, is Burnley!). He then talked about his happy years working for the Vicar, writing this newsletter and compiling his famous "dodgy dossiers"!

When it came to questions from the audience, there was an unfortunate moment when an elderly lady asked a question about the sad death of Dr Kelly, our local GP. All the audience cheered when Mr Campbell came back, quick as a flash, with the clever retort "F*** off, you stupid old bag". She was then escorted from the hall by Mr Kemp, amid laughter, to be given a savage mauling by Mr Blunkett's dog. A great evening was had by all.
A.C.

## Highlights of the Vicar's Latest Keynote Sermon on the Text 'The End Is Nigh'
### (Book of Justifications, 7.4)

Our enemies are everywhere. Who knows where they are or who they are? But they are someone. And they are evil. And they are there. There is no doubt that they are evil. And they are someone. And they are there. This is my message to you all. And when we find out who and where they are, then they will be brought to justice! Unless they are the wrong people then we will demand that they are sent home. Remember the text "Be not afraid. I am with you until the end of time. Which may be sooner than you think".

*The sermon can be read in full on the vicarage website www.dontpanic.com*

# IN YOUR ALLOTMENT
## With Mrs Beckett

I know that thousands of you have presented a petition to the vicarage against my decision to sow the St Albion's allotment with Mr Sainsbury's new genetically-modified Mackerel Maize. But I assure you all that you are completely wrong in your ridiculous Luddite prejudice against a product which has passed every scientific test. The maize is not only 100 percent safe but utterly delicious, tasting as it does of fish-fingers with a hint of amontillado sherry. Everyone will love it, especially the GM-jellyfish who will be free to nest in the 100-metre high maize forest, as it provides shelter for every kind of wildlife, from three-headed frogs to luminous wolves.

Incidentally, if anyone wishes to contact me on this or any other matter, I will be unavailable for the next three months, as I am going round the world in my caravan on a combined holiday and "save the planet" tour! M.B.

# Clarification

We recently reported on the talk given by Mr Campbell's partner, Ms Miller, under the title "Send your kids to f****** state schools, or else". We would like to make it clear that Ms Miller's reference to "hypocritical, middle-class parents who send their children to church schools" was in no way intended to be a criticism of the vicar and Ms Booth, who have every right to send their children to Our Lady Of The League Tables to ensure that they get a reasonable education. D.H.

#  Parish Postbag

Dear Sir,

I have the greatest possible respect for the Vicar's lawyer friend Mr Falconer. He may be a "cheeky chappy", but he is quite obviously stark, raving

Yours faithfully,
Screaming Lord Woolf,
The Old Woolsack, Lords Lane.

The Editor reserves the right to cut all letters disrespectful of Mr Falconer, the distinguished former flatmate and close personal friend of the Vicar. D.H.

# ST ALBION PARISH NEWS

## 2nd April 2004

*Buenos días!*

As I said to my new Spanish friend Brother Zapatero, when I had the pleasure of meeting him in Madrid last week!

Although we had never met before, and although he had accused me of being a liar, I am glad to say that we got on extremely well!

Indeed, he is now my closest friend, even though we disagree on a whole range of issues, such as whether or not I am a liar!

Still, I am sure you will agree that that made a very good start to our new friendship!

Unfortunately, I did not have any more time to spend with Fra Zapatero because I then had to "move on" to Libya. This is where I continued my inter-faith mission by meeting the spiritual leader of six million Libyans, Mahatma Ganddafhi.

I know a number of people in the parish have been unhappy about this, just as they were unhappy about our support for the Rev. Dubya's great crusade against the Evil One!

But to all those doubting Thomases (and Clares and Robins and all the others whose Christian names I have not got room to list here!) I say, "If we had not gone forth on our great campaign for world peace, would the Mahatma now be prepared to sit down with me in his tent, and offer me a dish of dried camel dung – which I am told is the greatest tribute any Arab host can pay to an honoured guest?" (See below for Mr de la Nougerede's marvellous illustration of the scene.)

And now, thanks to the success of our peace mission in Iraq, the great Mahatma has agreed to forswear the use of violence forever!

Truly he is a sinner who repenteth! And does not the Good Book tell us that, "There is more joy in

heaven over the sinner who is prepared to sell us oil than there is over the ninety-nine virtuous men who have nothing to offer"?
*(Book of Exxonus, 15.6)*

Adios amigos!

*Antonio*

---

 ## To Remember In Your Prayers

● The Rev. Kennedy, minister of the United Reform Liberal Democrat church, who, as you all know, is extremely ill. We have all been very shocked by Mr Kennedy's recent appearance and blurred speech, and we pray that he will find the strength to understand the real reasons for his illness. We pray that he will come to terms with his drink problem and realise that he is only resorting to alcohol because he is incapable of doing his job properly. Let's face it, leading a congregation is a very tough and demanding job, even if you aren't ill, which I am not, whatever Carole Caplin and the Queen may say! So please don't waste your time praying for me since I am 100 percent fit! So, we should all remember to pray for the Rev. Kennedy's early retirement, particularly when we recall his embarrassing efforts in recent months to criticise your vicar and our good friend the Rev Dubya for attempting to rid the world of evil. Now that we understand that Mr Kennedy only said these things because he was suffering from delirium tremens, hallucinations and all the other symptoms of what the doctors now know as "Mowlam's Syndrome By Proxy", we should all feel the appropriate degree of compassion, and hope that he has the good sense to retire before he dies! T.B.

---

 # Parish Postbag

*Dear Sir,*

*I would like to apologise for my very unfortunate and unforgiveable slip of the tongue when I inadverently referred to our treasurer Mr Brown as "the Vicar". I have no idea what came over me, since in recent months we have increasingly come to realise that there is only one man capable of giving this parish the leadership it needs and that is the Vicar, Mr Brown.*

*Yours faithfully,*
*Mrs Harman,*
*Two Sisters Road.*

# ═ Salve ═

**A** very warm welcome to Mr Howell James, who is going to be advising the Vicar over his relations with the "media". Mr James is of course an old friend of the parish, being a former "partner" of the current "partner" of our former churchwarden Mr Mandelson! What a small world it is, and what an amazing coincidence it is that I should have given him a job! I also gather that Mr James is a good friend of my friend Mr Birt, who is in charge of the PCC's "Blue Sky Thinking" department. What an even smaller world that makes it! T.B.

## Planning Notice:
## St Albion's District Council

A planning application has been submitted for the building of a 30-metre high concrete wall by the Sharon Construction Co (Tel Aviv) to surround the St Albion's vicarage and adjacent buildings. The purpose of this scheme is to protect the vicar and members of the PCC from the terrorist outrages which we are assured by Mr Blunkett of the Neighbourhood Watch are shortly to take place. Any objections must be registered with the Council by February 12 last year.

*J. Prescott, Chairman of the Planning Committee*

# MR CAMPBELL'S ONE MAN SHOW

**Alastair demonstrates how to present the truth in a straightforward and honest way!!
Tickets still available!!!!
P.M.**

# More Tea, Vicar?

You'd be amazed how much of the Vicar's time is spent drinking tea. Did you know:

Tony consumes 2,107 cups of tea every year!

This is a 12% increase on the tea consumption of any of his predecessors as Vicar!

Tony has promised to hit a target of 2,500 cups of tea within the next five years (bringing him into line with European Beverage Consumption averages)

The Vicar's favourite tea is English Breakfast Tea but he is equally fond of Scottish Breakfast Tea, Welsh Breakfast Tea and Northern Irish Breakfast Tea. (He strongly dislikes Earl Grey Tea because it is based on the hereditary principle and has not been chosen by him!)

Tony is equally happy drinking tea from a cup and saucer, or a mug. Just because one is considered 'middle class' and the other is supposedly 'working class', Tony sees no need to make a fuss. "Let's concentrate on the content", he says, "not on how it's presented!"

Drinking tea does *not* drive you mad – as claimed by those looking after poor old Mr Benn who certainly 'liked a drop'. However, this had nothing to do with his sad decline. In fact, tea makes you fit, strong, alert and ready to face the pressures of the toughest job there is – Vicar of St Albion's!

Time for another cup! D.H

# ST ALBION PARISH NEWS

*16th April 2004*

*Hullo!*

Easter is a very sad time, I always think, and never more so than this year, with the tragedy that has befallen my great friend Beverley Hughes.

You all know Bev. A finer servant to the parish it would be harder to imagine, and someone who, in her words, was the "most upright, honest, dedicated and competent member the PCC has ever had".

Nicely put, Bev!

And you ask any of the Romanian families who are camping out in the churchyard what they think of Bev!

They'll be the first to say that they had a real friend in Bev, who did so much to help them!

So why, you're asking, did Bev have to be "sacked"?

Well, hey, I feel a bit like one of the characters in the Easter story, which you've all been seeing in the cinema lately.

I'm talking about that much-maligned hero of the whole story, Pontius Pilate, who had to take some really tough decisions in order to keep the show on the road, and who has since had nothing but abuse from ignorant people who could not see how difficult his job was!

Remember when the mob was howling for Bev's blood, shouting, "Sack her, sack her!"?

It was then that I said that I could find no fault in her. "What has this woman done?" I asked.

"She's told a whole lot of lies!" they shouted. "But apart from that," I shouted down to them, "what else has Bev done?"

And you know, they had no reply! Which is why it is so sad that I had to sack her!

But, like poor old Pontius Pilate, I am "washing my hands" of this one! It's hardly my fault that I had to sack her, so I cannot be held responsible in anyway for her sad departure!

If anyone is to blame, it is probably Mr Blunkett, who runs the Neighbourhood Watch and is meant to be the first to notice when thousands of Romanians move in to live in the churchyard! See opposite for a picture!

I am second to none in my admiration for David, who has done a great job running our Neighbourhood Watch, with his much-loved dog Cerberus.

David has been an outstanding servant of the parish, in his tireless campaign to stamp out dangerous and old-fashioned ideas about "civil liberties", and to ensure that no foreign visitors could set up a campsite in the churchyard!

This is why I have decided to take over the Neighbourhood Watch myself, although of course David will still be very much in charge on a day-to-day basis!

As for Bev, I don't think we need to feel too sorry for her. One of the central messages of Easter, after all, is that people can come back again!

I am sure this will be as true for Bev as it has been for some of my other "disciples" in this parish – Peter, Stephen, Harriet, Estelle, and Peter again!

So on that note of "resurrection", I think we can now draw a line under anything that Bev or Mr Blunkett may or may not have done, and sing that greatest of all Easter hymns:

*"Move on, move on,*
*With hope in your heart!"*

Allelulia!

*Tony*

# Parish Scenes

**The Churchyard!!**
**By Local Artist Mr de la Nougerede**

## A Message from the Rev. Dubya, Chief Minister of the Church of the Latter-Day Morons

*To all my brothers and sisters in Englandland, greetings (and warnings!)*

In these last times, as it has been foretold, many shall rise up to bear false witness against me. Snakes and vipers shall crawl from under every stone. And one shall be called Judas Clarke, who will claim that, as the trumpet sounded in the hour of danger, I lay asleep in my tent and allowed the towers of the city to be razed by bin Laden and his gang of badhats and no-good hombres.

But, as Sister Condy has testified under solemn oath before the Church elders, there is no truthitude in the above tissue of false propheticness. I was not asleep. My six-guns were loaded, and ready to blaze away at the Great Satan skulking in his lair in Baghdad like a sick coyote. Yessir, and now another false prophet has arisen in the land, a snake-oil salesman from out East who calls himself Kerry. He *too* says that I was asleep on my watch when bin Laden was riding in.

But I say unto Kerry, this town ain't big enough for the both of us. Make your play, Kerry, and eat lead. Then we'll know who's the fastest gun in the West – Marshall Dubya, the Texas ranger, or the smooth-talking carpetbagger Kerry!

*Yours in the Lord! Rev. Dubya*

# Women's Groups

*Mrs Jowell writes:*

There was a special emergency meeting of all the parish Women's Groups last Tuesday, to demonstrate sisterly solidarity with Ms Hughes ('Our Bev' as we all know her) after the disgraceful decision by the vicar that she should be sacked from the PCC for telling lies. We all agreed that Bev had done nothing wrong, and even if she had, she is still a woman, which makes the vicar's action unforgivable. Once again this demonstrates that a woman can only get so far in the parish before she hits her head on the "glass ceiling" (or rather gets "hit on the head" by some aggressive member of the male-dominated parish establishment).

After the passing of this resolution, Ms Cherie Booth QC gave a short talk on "Why Women Should not be Sent to Prison and Men Should". She cited an interesting recent case where an Australian immigrant with a criminal record had embarrassed a very famous person and his wife and her friend. "Obviously," she said, "this man, whom I cannot name, but let us call him Mr Foster, should be gaoled for life and then deported. Furthermore he compounded his felony by publishing a book in order to make money, a clear infringement of the human rights of the Vicar and his family."

After the talk, Ms Carole Caplin served her own delicious home-made organic hot-cross buns from Sainsbury's. She very graciously declined any fee for the buns, but suggested instead that a token donation of £10 a head would be very welcome.

# ST ALBION PARISH NEWS

*30th April 2004*

*Hullo!*

And it seems that some people in the parish have had nothing better to do than to complain that I have done what they call a "u-turn" on the subject of the parish's role in the wider context of the European Church.

And what's wrong with that, I ask? Doesn't every sensible driver have to perform a u-turn occasionally, as conditions change?

If we see that we are coming up to roadworks, or that there is a pile-up on the road ahead, or that, heaven forbid, the road is leading straight over a cliff – then, hey, it would be quite wrong *not* to do a u-turn!

Not that in this case we were heading for a cliff! Don't get me wrong!

"But, Vicar," I hear some of the awkward squad saying in the pews at the back of the church, "didn't you make a point of saying, at the parish outing last year, that you didn't have a reverse gear?"

Firstly, can I say how sad it is that some of you have got nothing better to do than to dig around in old copies of the newsletter for things I said in the past, that you can then use to trip me up?

Honestly!

Secondly, can I just point out that, in order to do a u-turn, you do NOT NEED TO USE A REVERSE GEAR!

The whole point of doing a u-turn is that you continue to move forwards, not backwards, throughout the manoeuvre!

And that's precisely what I'm doing – continuing to move forward on the great motorway of life!

Was it not the Blessed Margaret herself who said, "You turn if you like, but I'm not going to"?

And if it was good enough for my great predecessor, the Deaconess Thatcher, then it's certainly good enough for me!

So that's why I am asking you all to move forward with me, in the opposite direction to which we were going, so that everyone in the parish can have the chance to give their views on this vital question of this parish's future role in the wider oecumenical European context that we all support!

When I was recently on a well-earned break in Bermuda (after my hugely successful half-hour visit to the Rev. Dubya at his Washington tabernacle), I decided that it was only right that you should all have the opportunity to support me in my plans to move ahead.

I knew that I could count on the full backing of the PCC, once they read about it in the local paper.

All it will involve is answering a simple "Yes" or "No" questionnaire, as below:

☐ YES, the Vicar is doing a marvellous job and we should all give him 100 percent support

☐ NO, I am an idiot and my views should be discounted

So, let the "ballot" commence!

Yours, in anticipation of victory!

Commander-in-Chief of "Operation Yes"!!!!

---

 # Parish Postbag
**From: Mr D. Desmond, ex-friend of the Vicar**

*Dear Sir,*

*Having supported the Vicar for quite a while now and having forked out very generously for the Vicar's "Gift Aid Scheme", I now wish to make clear that "enough is enough". And you know what I mean, Tony, because I told you when you had me round to the vicarage for tea with your wife and that sexy friend of hers, Carole, blimey, she'd look a bit of alright in one of my mags, perhaps I should start a new one specially for her, Holistic Babes, no offence Your Reverence, anyway, I digress, when I say "enough is enough", I'm talking about all them immigrants flooding into the parish and taking the jobs of decent, honest, hardworking purveyors of top-shelf adult entertainment, such as Asian*

*Yours faithfully,*
*D. Desmond,*
*Proprietor, Dirty Des's Mags 'n' Fags Emporium (above the chip shop), Filth Street.*

**The Editor regrets that some letters may have to be cut to avoid their authors being allowed to advertise their pornographic magazines in this family newsletter.** *D.H*

## A Letter from the Rev. Dubya

*Greetings to the Rev. Tiny Bloom*

It was a privilege and an honority to welcome you and your good lady Chardonnay, once again to my humble ranch, to chew over the next moves in our battle to rid the world of all these pesky new Satans who seem to have sprung up since we got rid of the old Great Satan who we found in that hole in the ground!

You Tiny, are the one 'stand-up guy' who has backed me through thick and thin while every other coyote and rattlesnake has run off with his tail between his legs, like this new hombre from Spainland, Senor Yellowbolero or whatever he calls himself. But I tell you, he won't get away with it, no sir! There's no sombrero big enough for him to hide under!

But Tiny, you and I ride on together, to finish the job that we started! They'll try to ambush us at the creek, sure they will! They'll try to head us off at the pass, sure they will! They'll shoot us in the ass, even if we're dead, sure they will! But do we give a damn, no sirree!

*Yours in the Lord! Rev. Dubya*

The vicar's wife and Rev. Dubya's wife join together in a chorus of the old American classic (!!!!!) at an informal karaoke service during the vicar's trip to Washington. D.H.

# ST ALBION PARISH NEWS

*14th May 2004*

*Hullo!*

And we've recently been celebrating a very special day!

Obviously, I don't just mean my birthday – although, of course, that was a pretty special day!

And can I just say a big thank you to all those parishioners who sent me cards, presents and flowers!

It is a great shame that they must all have got lost in the post! And, don't worry, I'll be taking that one up at the very highest level with the postman, if he ever dares show his face around here again!

No – what, of course, we've all been celebrating and giving thanks for is the 25th anniversary of that shining inspiration to us all, the Blessed Margaret.

For some of the children who may not know the story – and even for some of the grown-ups who may have forgotten – let me just remind you of the remarkable contribution she made to the life of our parish.

Born in a humble corner shop hundreds of years ago, she rose to become the first woman priest to be put in charge of St Albion's.

And, by golly, didn't she change everything for ever!

Who will forget the moment when she first arrived on the doorstep of the vicarage, the light creating a supernatural halo around her head, and adapted those famous words of St Francis of Sinatra, "I'm going to do it my way"!

Of course, there were plenty of people – and there still are – who said that the Deaconess was difficult to live with and work for!

But saints, by their very nature, are difficult people. They upset people by telling the truth!

They annoy people by being right all the time!

They have the courage to do things that other people are too scared or cowardly to do!

Hey, I'm no saint (not yet at least!), but people say the same thing of me. He's difficult, they say. He just wants to do everything *his* way, they say. I've even heard one or two people saying "he's mad"!

But that's exactly what they used to say about the Blessed Margaret (before, sadly, she went mad and had to be burned at the stake!).

But all that is behind us now, as we demonstrated when we

consecrated our new Iron Lady Chapel, with that wonderful statue by Mr Nougerede. The event was only slightly marred by the very curious antics of our local solicitor, Mr Howard, who has recently settled in the parish after emigrating from Transylvania.

It was a great shame that he should have chosen this particular solemn occasion to shout out that he actually knew the Blessed Margaret, and that she had annointed **him** to be her representative on earth!

Talk about mad! Who's the madman here? If anyone's mad, it's him, Mr Howard!

He's mad, Mad, MAD! Do you hear?

Yours going for a lie-down,

Tony

**The new Iron Lady Chapel with the statue by local sculptor Mr Nougerede!**

# Get Fit For Summer!!!

**With Charles Clarke, Chairman of the Governors of St Albion's Technology, Skills and Lifelong Learning Beacon College (formerly the Herbert Morrison Comprehensive)**

*Mr Clarke writes:*

*We all owe it to the Vicar to keep as fit and slim as possible. Don't get me wrong! You don't need to go to the gym to spend hours on a bicycling machine!*

*You don't have to give up eating your favourite burgers and fries!*

*Just try this simple exercise routine, which will soon pay handsome dividends when it comes to the feel-good factor!*

## Day One

1. Take a leisurely walk down to the polling station.
2. Place a cross next to the word 'Vicar'.
3. Walk home again.

*Estimated calorie loss: up to 16,000.*

## Start today the Charlie Clarke way!

*Watch out for more tips next week!*

## A Message from Rev. Dubya Bush of the Church of the Latter-Day Morons

Brothers and Sisters in Albionland, it grieves me sorely to tell you that one of my trusted pastors, Brother Rumsfeld, has confessed to grave misdoingtudes and grievous errornesses which have brought our mission in Iraq into serious disreputability!

But rest assured, my Bretheren Across the Bay, I have rebuked Brother Rumsfeld for his transgressuals and for his falling into the hands of the evil one who lurketh who knoweth where.

And the sinner Rumsfeld hath repentethed and in is now in a state of penitude.

And so I have forgiven him, as the *Book of Revelations in the New Yorker* says, "There is more rejoicing in heaven over one sinner that repenteth than ninety-nine Iraqis tortured to death".

*Praise be to the Lord! Alleluia!*

# THE POWER OF PRAYER

**Brother Rumsfeld says: "I'm sorry... I was caught!!" T.B.**

# PCC Elections

This year we have introduced a very important change in the arrangements for our parish elections. I know many of you have been concerned at the low turnouts in recent years, because people were so happy with the way the parish was being run that they didn't need to go down to the primary school to put their X next to the Vicar's name! But now, in an effort to give the young people of the parish a sense that they too can participate in the running of parish affairs, we have decided to lower the voting age to five. Now all the members of our Sunday School can feel really involved, though we will have to keep the voting form simple!

I have, therefore, drafted this easy-to-use voting form, which even the smallest toddler will be able to understand!

---

### Do you like the Vicar?

| Yes |
|-----|
| Yes |

Just tick one box (or both if you want!)

---

And, don't worry, even if you lose your voting slip, under our new postal ballot system we'll still count that as a 'yes' vote!

And just to encourage everyone, the children will be singing this new version of a favourite old song, with Mrs Hodge at the electric keyboard:

> *Boys and girls come out to vote,*
> *Grab your hat and grab your coat,*
> *Leave your telly and your mobile phone,*
> *Here's your chance to vote for Tone.*

Let's make sure we all join in, shall we children? T.B.

# ST ALBION PARISH NEWS

*28th May 2004*

*Hullo!*

I am sure we all remember that wonderful story in the Bible about the brave boy who stood on the burning deck and refused to leave his ship while everyone was diving overboard and swimming away?

Does that remind you of anyone? Can any of the children tell me? Yes, Rashid, you've got your hand up and, of course, it's me, isn't it? Your vicar. Obviously I'm not on a sinking ship, and it's not burning either! In fact, the ship is sailing along perfectly happily and making very good time, thank you very much, with a full cargo and a fair wind!

But that hasn't stopped Mr Prescott taking the only lifeboat and rowing away with his friend Mr Brown.

I am still not quite sure why I, as your vicar, wasn't invited on their little outing to Iona, to visit the shrine of St John the Smith.

As it happened, I couldn't have gone on their ridiculous little pilgrimage anyway, because I had to be in Turkey attending an interfaith outreach workshop with our Moslem brothers.

Still, it would have been nice to have been asked! But don't think I'm getting at you, John and Gordon, just because you've been talking about me behind my back while you stuff oysters into your faces in some Scottish car park!

Oh, yes, I know what you've both been up to! Nothing escapes me, you know!

But don't worry! We believe in free speech in this parish!

If Mr Prescott wants to talk a lot of rubbish about "shifting plates" of food down his gullet, then he's perfectly free to do so!

And if Mr Brown's got nothing better to do than listen to this sort of nonsense when he should be concentrating on the parish finances, then that's fine by me!

Hey, I don't even mind if someone throws a bag of flour at me when I'm trying to preach a sermon, as happened at last week's Evensong!

Some people, particularly our local solicitor Mr Howard and his friends, got in a bit of a panic and ran for the doors.

But I didn't! No, I just stood there, like that boy on the burning deck, because I know that this sort of thing comes with the territory!

All great preachers have had to put up with people throwing things at them during the service, and I'd much rather have to cope with a bag of purple flour than a silly interruption from Mr Howard!

But, joking apart, I have been advised that to stop this kind of nonsense occurring again, we will have to speed up our plans to build a 20-foot-high security wall round the pulpit, and in the meantime I will be conducting all services via an interactive video link from our new studio in the crypt!

For security reasons, there will be no congregation in the crypt and any cars attempting to park in the precincts of the church will be made subject to a controlled explosion!

I didn't want to do this, guys, but our new security adviser Mr Scarlett (who is a friend of Mr Campbell, and you can't get a much higher recommendation than that!) has insisted on tightening up all our arrangements, on the grounds that we can expect an attack on the church within 45 minutes!

But despite being left alone to cope with all these difficulties, you will be comforted to know that my resolve to carry on is stronger than ever.

You chose me in 1997 to do a job and, hey, I'm going to finish it!

In the words of the late Blessed St Margaret,

**HOW IT WILL LOOK:**
**Local architect Alan de la Nougerede's sketch for the proposed pulpit security screen**

just before she was led out and burned at the stake, "I fight on, and I fight to win"!

I've even written a chorus which I will have to sing on my own at evensong in the crypt:

*"Fight on, fight on, there's a job to be done,
Fight on, fight on, there's a war to be won"* (repeat)

Yours,

*Tony*

---

 Readers Postbag

**From the Former Editor of the Newsletter, Mr Campbell**

*Dear Sir,*

*I am reliably informed that people in the parish AT A HIGH LEVEL are putting it about that whilst working for the vicar I was some kind of bloody LOOSE CANNON and had to be restrained by the bloody VICAR NO LESS!!!*

*If I find out who these people are I shall personally go round to their houses and smash their ****ing*

**(This letter has been edited as unsuitable for a family newsletter T.B.)**

---

✝ *To Remember In Your Prayers*

● Rev. Dubya Bush of the Church of the Latter-Day Morons who has fallen off his bicycle and sustained multiple grazes to his hand and chin. O Lord, let us pray that this great and good man is granted a speedy recovery and a new bicycle and let us also give thanks for the vicar's deliverance from his assailants armed with flour. We are asked to forgive our enemies but in this case we won't. T.B.

---

## Poet's Corner

*Verses by a local writer, 'Gordie', in memory of the late John Smith*

### The Lost Leader

You never lived to see this day,
The church you loved has lost its way.
If only you had been our leader
Instead of this stupid bleeder,
He would have done the job much better
And yet

**This poem has been cut for obvious reasons.
D. Hill, Acting Editor, St Albion's Parish Newsletter**

# ST ALBION PARISH NEWS
## 11th June 2004

*Hullo!*

As you may know, this is a very historic week in the life of the parish!

No, not those silly little elections which some parishioners seem to find so exciting, like Mr Silk and the elderly Miss Collins, who I saw making a fool of herself the other day, driving down the High Street in her Rolls, waving to everyone.

No, what I'm talking about is much more important and historic than that!

Can any of the children tell me what happened 60 years ago this week?

Hamsa, you've got your hand up. No, not the foundation of a Zionist state in Israel, although that was a good guess! I'm talking about D-Day, when British and American forces, together in a coalition, had the courage to invade another country which was suffering under an evil tyrant with a moustache!

Does that ring any bells, children? Do you see any parallels with today? I know that's a long word to use in this newsletter, but it comes from the Greek *'para'*, meaning airborne assault troops, and *'lell'*, meaning going into hell for the sake of democracy!

So, I'm celebrating not just the old D-Day, when we won such a glorious victory, but the new D-Day (or 'Dubya Day' as I believe we should call it) which I am sure in the end will be seen as a victory just as glorious!

Am I right in thinking that if Mr Cook and Mrs Short and all those other embittered former members of the PCC had been around in the 1940s, they would have been on Mr Hitler's side? (No offence, guys, but it's true, isn't it?)

And here's another thought. In those days we were really serious when we said that we wanted to be at the heart of Europe! (Mr Howard, please note.)

But that's probably enough of going down memory lane!

The sort of history I am interested in is in the future, not the past!

And I've still got a job to do here, whatever the gossip may be in the Working Men's Club when John stands Gordon a pint of – what is it they drink down there? – bitter, I expect!

After they've had a few, they get silly and start talking about who's going to be vicar next!

But I want everyone in the parish to know once and for all that I've got that job to do, and I'm going to see it through, however long it takes.

I've even composed a chorus which I hope you will all enjoy singing at next week's Evening Service (when, alas, I won't be able to be with you, because I have to be abroad on one of my many outreach missions to bring the message of peace to all mankind – after all, wasn't that the whole point of our great Middle East crusade in the first place?).

These are the words:

*I've got a job to do,*
*I'm going to see it through.*
*I give this pledge to you,*
*Let's all do it too.*

(Words and music T. Blair)

Yours for ever and ever, amen!

*Tony*

(Not forgetting the women, of course – thanks for reminding me, Cherie!)

# Memories of D-Day

**The vicar and Cherie attend a special service to celebrate victory in Europe!**

# St Albion's Goes Interactive!!!

## Your chance to put your questions directly to the vicar!

**Q:** Vicar, I am deeply concerned about the recent deaths of servicemen at our local training camp. Don't you think that you should look into this tragedy?

***The Vicar writes:*** May I say that no one is more sorry about these events than me, and I would like to begin by offering my heartfelt condolences to all those who have lost loved ones in this very sad episode.

**Q:** Vicar, I am deeply concerned about the growing number of servicemen who are being killed in Iraq. Would it be right to send out more of them?

***The Vicar writes:*** May I say that no one is more sorry about these events than me, and I would like to begin by offering my heartfelt condolences to all those who have lost loved ones in this very sad episode.

**Q:** Does the Vicar think it is morally right for local train drivers to go on strike on the day of the elections?

***The Vicar writes:*** May I say that no one is more sorry about these events than me, and I would like to offer my heartfelt condolences to all those who

***The Editor writes:*** For space reasons we'll have to leave it there, but our thanks to all those parishioners who have taken part in this very important exercise in parish democracy.

 # Parish Postbag

*Dear Sir,*

*I was really angry when I drove into the forecourt of our local Tesco 24/7 filling station to see that a litre of unleaded petrol had gone up to 109p. Who are we to blame for this catastrophic rise? My own view is that the fault lies with all those who kept preaching sanctimonious sermons about the need for armed intervention in the Middle*

*Yours sincerely,*
*Gordon Brown.*

*(Please note change of address: from September I will be moving to The Vicarage, St Albion's)*

**The Editor writes: Letters may be cut for reasons of space or blatant disloyalty.**

# ST ALBION PARISH NEWS

### 25th June 2004

## *Stand Up, Stand Up For Tony!!!*

### A Message To All Parishioners
### From Peter Mandelson

YES, it's a totally new look for your parish newsletter this week. And no apologies for that!

In the light of some very cruel and unnecessary things that have been said about the Vicar recently, Tony has called me in to spell out a few home truths!

Some of you don't seem to have grasped just how serious the situation here at St Albion's has become.

I've heard people who ought to know better saying that the Vicar has lost his grip. That he is tired and worn out. Even that he has become mentally unbalanced.

What if he has? The point is that Tony is our Vicar, and far and away the best Vicar we've ever had, and ever could have.

That is why, all those years ago, I was the one who first saw his potential and put him where he is today.

Just think of all the good things which Tony has achieved in the past seven years. I am sure we all have our own list of what he has done for the parish in that time.

Some might, for instance, point to our wonderful parish celebrations for the Millennium, centred round that unforgettable Tent (still, incidentally, for sale – see parish website for details).

Others might recall the success of our mission to Northern Ireland, in which I was privileged to play the central role (forgive me for blowing my own trumpet, but that has to be one of our finest achievements!).

But all that aside, let's look at the man himself.

Let me just give one instance of why Tony stands head and shoulders above us all.

As you know, some years back, when I was your churchwarden, I got into a bit of a tangle over my mortgage.

Thanks to the vindictive attitude of the previous editor of this newsletter, Mr Campbell, it was thought wise that I should take a back seat for a while in the running of the parish – which I was very happy to do since, although I had done nothing wrong, my sole wish was not to embarrass the Vicar.

Then it happened again. There was a silly misunderstanding over some help I gave to one of our most generous local benefactors, Mr Hinduja.

Again, the embittered and twisted Mr Campbell saw this as an opportunity to make me a scapegoat. And, once again, in deference to the interests of Tony, I was prepared to keep a low profile!

It was entirely predictable that, sooner or later, Mr Campbell would overreach himself and start behaving as if he was the most important person in the parish.

And if the Vicar has now become unpopular, who is there to blame other than the power-crazed psychopath who is now reduced to travelling round tatty little provincial theatres, telling everyone what a great man he is!

The fact that nobody goes to see him making such a sorry exhibition of himself in this fashion simply demonstrates how wrong he is!

Now we can draw a line under Mr Campbell, who has left the vicarage in such a shambles.

Fortunately, the Vicar has got one person on whose unfailing support he can always count, which is why he has called me back in his hour of need.

Try to imagine just what it would be like if Tony was to heed all those deranged parishioners (even including several ex-members of the PCC) who are calling for him to step down.

For a start, I know that I myself would be out of a job, and many others would too.

It is hard to conceive just what chaos would ensue for the parish.

Walls covered with graffiti. Teenagers drunkenly roaming the streets. Parishioners terrified to go out at night, for fear of being mugged.

So let me just say a final word to those of you who may not have understood the gravity of what I am saying.

*I know where you live!*

**Thank you for your attention.**
**Peter Mandelson**
**Camp Commandant**

# A (brief!) note from Tony

*A*s you know, I have had to be abroad rather a lot recently, attending various important meetings and conferences in Europe. And that's why I've had to ask Mr Mandelson to step in, to keep the show on the road back here in the parish!

I only want to make one point to you all this week, in answer to what our former organist Mr Cook and others have been saying. That is that I should apologise to the whole parish for getting it wrong in supporting the Rev. Dubya's crusade against the Evil One.

Of course I believe that we all have a duty to say that we are sorry when we have genuinely done something wrong. And I can assure you all that if, for instance, I had betrayed my wife and been caught misbehaving with my secretary in the organ loft, I might well feel constrained to make a grovelling confession!

But as far as the Rev. Dubya's great battle against Satan is concerned, I think you all know in your hearts that history will eventually prove that we were right!

Sorry, Robin, but I'm not going to say "sorry". Shall we leave it there and move on?

Yours in haste (or wherever I am at the moment!),

*Tony*

## A Declaration Of Support From Our Treasurer Mr Brown

*Dear Sir,*

*I would like at this time to put on record my full support for the Vicar. Over the last seven years, he has done a magnificent job, which in years to come he can look back on with great pride. I am sure we can all wish him well in his new*

*Yours sincerely,*
*Gordon Brown,*
*C/o Bishops Move.*

**The editor reserves the right to cut all letters for reason of space.**

# A SIGN OF PIECE
## (of paper)

The vicar returning from his European mission, waving a
piece of paper signed by all the spiritual leaders –
promising that St Albion's will be entirely free to run its
own affairs (provided that its decisions are in agreement
with what the European churches have already laid out).
Quite a coup! By local artist Mr de la Nougerede

# ST ALBION PARISH NEWS

*9th July 2004*

*Hullo!*

I wonder how many of you can name the ten commandments, without looking them up?

Obviously I can, because I'm the vicar!

And I expect most of you can do the easy ones, such as "thou shalt not kill" and "thou shalt not commit adultery" (no need to remind our former organist Mr Cook about that one!).

But a lot of people tend to overlook the most important commandment of all – the one which says "thou shalt not covet thy neighbour's job".

And who is our neighbour? It's easy, isn't it children?

It's the man who lives next door to you. In, say, my case, that would be Mr Brown, wouldn't it?

Now I'm not saying that Mr Brown is in any way trying to get my job, any more than I am trying to get his! (with the parish finances in their current state, that would be a pretty silly thing to want, wouldn't it?!).

But if Mr Brown was being covetous, that would be very wrong, wouldn't it? "Sinful" even, to use an old-fashioned word that we don't hear much nowadays.

Surely the message is that we all of us have our own job to do in this life, which has been ordained for us, and which we go on doing, to the best of our abilities, for the rest of our lives!

In my case, obviously, it's being your vicar, and so long as I am "fit and well", as Mr Blunkett of the Neighbourhood Watch so succinctly put it last week, then there is no reason why I should not go on doing it for many years to come!

In Mr Brown's case, naturally, the same is true – unless of course he suffers some kind of breakdown, which can happen when a man spends too much time coveting his neighbour's job!

Sorry, but that's the truth of it, which is why the wise men of old, as we read in the Good Book, made it one of the deadly sins!

It drives you mad, and you start getting worked up and bitter about not getting the job which you were never qualified for in the first place, and which I only mentioned to you in that restaurant all those years ago to make you feel better about yourself because I was the one who was going to be vicar and not you!

But seriously, can you imagine Gordon standing shoulder to

shoulder with the Rev. Dubya, and bringing peace to the whole world?

No, it's laughable, isn't it? Gordon is fine so long as he sticks to what he's good at, poring over the parish accounts (though goodness knows how he'll cope now he hasn't got his clever young friend Mr Balls to tell him what to do!).

So, thanks to Mr Blunkett for bringing up that commandment as a parish talking point!

And let's quote it in full one last time shall we, so that everyone gets the message:

"Thou shalt not covet thy neighbour's job, nor his popularity, nor his superior abilities, nor his charisma, nor his boyish good looks, nor his charming and successful wife, nor anything that he hath." *(Book of Numbers, 10 and 11)*

Yours in power! Tony

# Parish Scenes

**The highlight of this year's Fête! Captured by local artist Mr de la Nougerede**

## For those who missed it –

*Mr Campbell's new interview show "Meet Alastair" on St Albion's Hospital Radio got off to a terrific start when he interviewed the former churchwarden Mr Mandelson. Here is a transcript of their fascinating encounter on the airwaves:*

**AC:** Thanks for coming on the show, Peter.

**PM:** It's my pleasure, Alastair.

**AC:** Do you think the vicar is doing a marvellous job?

**PM:** I do. And so is Mr Brown.

**AC:** I'm sorry. My headphones appear to be faulty. Did you say Mr Brown was doing a good job?

**PM:** Yes, the vicar asked me to put in a good word for Gordon who is the natural man to take over when Tony retires in twenty or so years' time. If he's still alive.

**AC:** You mean "If Tony is still alive"?

**PM:** No... Gordon. Because he's not a well man is he? Working so hard on those accounts...

**AC:** Ha, ha, ha.

**PM:** Ha, ha, ha, ha.

**AC:** Thank you so much. Now for my next record "Gordon is a Moron" by Jilted John Smith.

---

## A Message from Rev. Dubya Bush of the Church of the Latter-Day Morons

*Hosallelujah!*

Rejoice, brothers and sisters in the Lord! For today dawneth the dawn of a new dawn!

Today freedom has come to the people of Iraq-land, they who for so long have lived in slavery and darkness!

Today they have once again been given back the priceless gifts of libertation and democritude!

And, above all, we today see the Evil One himself standing in the dark and facing the Day of Judgement. The guy with the black hat has been rounded up by the guy in the white hat with his sheriff's star on his fancy weskit a glintin' in the sun ! *(That's me folks.)*

And can you hear that hammerin' from outside the window of the courthouse? Yessir, they're building the gibbet where they're going to hang him high like the no-good horse thief he is!

All that we predicted has come to pass, just as I and Brother Rumsfeld and Sister Condy prophesied. I don't want to say "I told you so" but "I foretold you so!"

Signed *Rev Dubya Bush.*
*(Texas Ranger First Class and US Marshal, Dodge City)*

# ST ALBION PARISH NEWS

*23rd July 2004*

*Hullo!*

I wonder if you can guess what I've been thinking about this week?

I've been mulling over my favourite book!

No, not Harry Potter, Rashid! Nor even the Koran!

It's from a book that not many people read nowadays, but which has got a lot of very interesting and relevant – and yes, modern things to say, even though it was written hundreds of years ago.

I'm talking, of course, about the Bible, which comes from the Greek Biblios, which means 'bestseller'!

Anyway, the text in question runs "We're left with three important concepts: good faith, hope and charity. And the most important of these is good faith". *(New Labour Bible, St Paul's Letter to the Joint Intelligence Committee.)*

You see, what I'm getting round to is the fact that, if you look hard enough, you can always find something in the Bible that is precisely relevant to your own situation!

And that phrase "good faith" is exactly what Mr Butler has now decided was the key to why I led the parish in joining the Rev Dubya's great crusade against the Evil One.

Look, Mr Butler had some pretty tough things to say about my sermons on the crusade!

And I respect him for that! He even says that I might have made some mistakes (although, as it happens, he ends up by agreeing that I didn't!).

Mr Butler has served St Albion's loyally ever since he left school in 1940 – he's that grey-haired man you see changing the altar cloths on Saturday mornings – and has been tireless in his support for many previous incumbents, including the Rev. Major and Deaconess Thatcher. So he's hardly the man to pull his punches when it comes to criticising the way we do things, is he?

That's why I don't mind admitting that I was a bit nervous when Mr Butler brought his report around to the vicarage and asked me if it was alright!

But I needn't have worried. Mr Butler has produced a marvellous piece of work – fair, balanced and thoughtful.

I could not have written it better myself!

And above all it contained that wonderful phrase, echoing the text I quoted earlier, "the vicar acted at all times and in every respect in good faith".

I can't think of a finer tribute to your vicar! In fact I wouldn't mind having those words written on my gravestone – when the time comes, of course, which won't be for a long time, because I'm very healthy, as you all saw when I was photographed in the St Albion's Fun Run, to raise money for Mr Prescott's exciting plan to build affordable houses on the school playing fields!

In fact, now I mention it, there is still one plain window in the church, the one above the altar, which really could benefit from having a proper stained glass picture in it.

I have asked our local artist Mr de la Nougerede to rough out a design, round that text which I keep mentioning, and which could serve to inspire generations of future St Albion worshippers!

Yours in good faith,

Tony

PS. If I have just one tiny little bone to pick with Mr Butler's otherwise faultless report, it is his suggestion that I make all my decisions sitting on the sofa at the vicarage with Mr Campbell and Mr Mandelson, instead of having formal discussions round a table with all the members of the PCC.

Well, of course, I wish we still had the luxury of doing it that way, but times have changed, the world has moved on!

Just think how long all that sort of thing used to take, listening to Mr Cook or Mrs Short holding forth at length and raising points of order!

How can you get anything done that way, in the age of the mobile telephone and the internet?

Honestly, the church could be burning down and Mr Brown could still be sitting there at the end of the table with a grumpy expression, asking if I knew what I was doing!

No, Mr Butler, it's a nice idea, but the sofa is the way forward! As we say nowadays, the sofa is the new church hall!

PPS. I forgot to mention that I have composed a new chorus, which will be given its "premier" at our evening service on Sunday:

*"Good faith, good faith,*
*He acted in good faith.*
*Good faith, good faith,*
*It's what the Good Book saith."*

 ## Millennium Tent Update

■ There is some very good news about the Millennium Tent which, as parishioners may recall, has not found a new use since our celebrations in 2000 (at a cost unfortunately, of £8 billion to parish funds).

We have now had an offer from a very respectable South African company, run by Mr Hendrik van der Kroek, which wants to resurrect the tent as an international gaming centre, thus adding immeasurably to the cultural life of the parish. Mr Van der Kroek, who has wide experiences of leisure promotions in Bonkinansawana, plans to re-christen our facility as "Sin City".

## Mr Blunkett of the Neighbourhood Watch

From now on I will be on the lookout for anyone stirring up religious hatred. For example, if someone were to say "Oi! The vicar is a load of rubbish", he would be arrested at once and then imprisoned for a long period for offending the faith of a large number of devout believers including myself. DB.

# Kiddiez Korner!

For all the children we've put together a special kidz-friendly version of Mr Butler's report. There's no need for any colouring in! Unless you've got a white crayon!

> ### Mr Butler's Report in Full

## PARISH ACCOUNTS

*We are obviously very grateful to our Treasurer Mr Brown for all the time he has put in on his spending plans for the next three years. Sadly, there is not room in this issue (or any subsequent ones) to publish his accounts in detail (or indeed at all!). I am sure it is all very interesting, and no doubt Gordon has done a thorough job, as always, but really there are more important things for us all to worry about than whether Gordon has got his figures right! If anyone's really bothered, the details are now available on the church website at www.boringstuff.stalbs.co.uk*

# ST ALBION PARISH NEWS

*6th August 2004*

*Hullo!*

And isn't it good that the sun's shining at last, just as I said it would!

As you know, Cherie and I and the family are taking a well-earned break in Barbados, thanks to the generous hospitality of that long-time friend of the parish Cliff Richard (who sang in our choir back in the 1950s, and whose faith has been a shining example to us all for so many decades)!

Before I pack my bags, I would like just to say a word or two about Mr Mandelson's new appointment as the parish's representative on the steering committee of the European Interpastoral Union.

There has been, I know, a good deal of misunderstanding about the reasons behind my decision to send Peter on this very important mission which, for a while, will take him out of the day-to-day life of the parish.

Some parishioners have got the idea that Peter and I both wished for him to be reinstated on the PCC, where he could have played a key part in shaping our exciting five-year plan to revitalise the parish.

According to these gossips and rumour-mongers, Peter's return to the PCC was only frustrated when at an angry meeting the rest of the PCC, led by Mr Prescott and Mr Straw, threatened to resign if our former churchwarden was brought back to his former role sitting next to me at PCC meetings and telling me what to do.

What nonsense! Peter has always been very popular with the PCC, even among those who do not like or trust him!

No, the reason for his new appointment is that he is quite simply THE BEST MAN FOR THE JOB, as he himself has so often pointed out! So, let's put an end to all this silly tittle-tattle, shall we, and draw a line under the malicious gossip.

It is time to move on, and I hope that when I come back from my working holiday, parishioners will have pulled themselves together and found something rather more important to occupy their minds than engaging in unhelpful speculation about the man I am pleased to call "Peter, my rock".

Yours, in holiday mood!

*Tony*

# A Statement From Mr Mandelson

As the Vicar has made clear, I am very happy to take up my very challenging new post in Belgium, acting on behalf of the parish. I am not surprised that the Vicar's courageous and eminently sensible decision has excited such an outburst of envious spite and malevolence from the usual suspects here at St Albion's. I am not going to glorify them by mentioning their names, but Mr Straw and Mr Kilfoyle will know who I mean!

Let the little people sneer! I have become well used over the years to hearing this kind of bitchy backbiting about all my efforts to help the Vicar. But I want you all to know that I am big enough to let this kind of thing not bother me in the slightest.

That is why I propose to take absolutely no notice of what these people are saying. It is simply what I have come to expect, and nothing whatever would be gained by my attempting to answer these pathetic slurs in this newsletter.

I will merely point out that, as the Vicar has made clear, I am simply the best qualified person to take on this job.

I have long been the foremost champion of our involvement in this great oecumenical experiment, and I can't think of anyone better to put the point of view of St Albion's to our European brethren.

But I would like to make one final point.

Although I naturally welcome my new appointment, and Reinaldo and I intend to take the fullest advantage of our time together in the lovely city of Brussels, I wish to emphasise that my new job is only a temporary one.

I will be keeping in very regular contact with the Vicar, to discuss parish matters, and in due course I have every intention of returning to my proper place on the PCC.

Meanwhile, I want you all to remember that I know where you live. OK?

### Peter Mandelson,

*Temporary Address: Rue des Matelots 41, Bruxelles, Belgium.*

# DATES FOR YOUR DIARY

Coming this autumn:

The Roy Jenkins Lecture

(Church Hall, October 7)

## 'The Sinning Sixties – Where Did We All Go Wrong?'

The Vicar will look back to the decade which, as he says, "led us all astray". He will explain why everything that is wrong in the parish, from graffiti on the Millennium Tent to the Dirty Des Mags and Video Emporium behind the chip shop in the High Street, can be blamed on the 1960s.

One definitely not to miss!

*Tickets available from Mrs Jowell, Chair of the PCC Sub-Committee on Culture, Sport and Leisure Activities.*

### Important Notice:

In future, no cakes or refreshments will be available at parish events, in accordance with the advice of the parish's "all powerful" Health and Safety Committee!

# Thank you, John!

A big thank you to our faithful security officer John Scarlett for all his diligent work in protecting the parish. John gets a lot of flak and people say he just does what I tell him. But, hey, what's wrong with that? (T.B)

# ST ALBION PARISH NEWS
## 20th August 2004

*Calamari!* (Which is the word for 'hullo' here in Greece, where Cherie and I are privileged to be attending the opening of the Olympic Games!)

And how appropriate that the Games should have come back to where they began, in the wonderful old city of Athens, birthplace of democracy!

And aren't the Games great? You know, there are some people back home who disapprove of competitive games!

You know the type I mean. They don't like School Sports Days. They want to ban the egg-and-spoon race at the village fete.

They can't bear anything that shows one person as better than another at anything.

But, hey, isn't that what life's all about?

Aren't we all engaged in a race of some kind with those around us?

If there's only one seat left on the bus, don't we all rush to get it first?

What's it the Good Book says? "The first shall be first and the last shall be last" *(Guinness Book of Records, 4.17).*

We all know people who are losers in this life – and what a bitter, twisted lot they are!

I'm sure you can all think of examples, even in our own parish! People who dropped out of the race when they saw that they weren't getting anywhere – and now stand on the sidelines, jeering, as they watch the winner proudly breasting the tape!

But then there is also the other type of

# VICAR LUDORUM!

**Local artist Mr De La Nougerede captures all the excitement of the vicar's trip to Athens!**

competitor who tries very hard – does all the training, works away round the clock, but just doesn't quite have that extra something special that separates the gold medallist from the Scottish bloke who is doomed always to come second!

No – give me a winner any day! And best of all, the guy who can win gold, and then come back four years later to win another, and who knows, even a third in a row!

That would be something truly Olympian, wouldn't it?

There's something for you all to ponder on in the coming days, as you sit at home watching the drama of the Athens Olympics unfolding on your television screens, while I am lucky enough to be seeing it live with the Chief Archimandrite and my other oecumenical brethren!

*Taramasalata!* (as they say here instead of 'goodbye'!)

Tony

---

# Congratulations!

The vicar would like to offer his blessing to Mr Blunkett and his new lady companion.

Although the lady appears to be married, they are both adults and what they do in the privacy of their own home office is up to them.

It's their own affair!

Those members of the congregation who have been quoting back at me my sermon about "the decadent morality of the 1960s" have totally misunderstood the point I was trying to make and they should be ashamed of themselves – *T.B.*

---

## TEXT FOR THE DAY
"It is more blessed to receive than to give".
*(Phreebees, 7.3)*
Perhaps some of the more envious members of the parish could think about this one over the holiday period! T.B

# Attention All Mums And Dads!!!

## An Urgent Message From Mrs Hodge, Our Parish Child Protection Coordinator

All parents are invited to the compulsory summer school in Parenting Skills, where experts on childcare, led by myself, will give instruction to all of you on where you are going wrong in bringing up your kids.

**Subjects will include:**

**1**. Am I middle-class, and what can I do about it?

**2**. Dads – get off your mobile, give up your job and spend some quality time at home with the kids!

**3**. Mums – stop hanging around at home and get out to work! (This course has been temporarily dropped from the curriculum.)

**4**. Kids – know your rights! Are your parents telling you what to do? If so, you could be entitled to compensation! Ring in confidence Childcash, Matrix Chambers, C/o Ms Booth QC, The Vicarage, and you could win a huge cash pay-out and/or see your parents in gaol!

● *Remember – attendance at these courses is mandatory for all adults, regardless of gender, sexual orientation or ethnic affiliation.*

● *Excuses from parents such as "lack of childcare" will **not** be accepted. Dump the kids with someone and turn up!*

Mrs Jowell is looking for volunteers to help with the refreshments.

Sorry, but once again we must remind you that homemade cakes or sandwiches are no longer permissible under health and safety rules; but any contributions bought direct from our friend Mr Sainsbury's shop in the High Street have been "vetted" as entirely acceptable.

Particularly recommended are his new GM salmon-flavoured scones!

# A Message From Mr Prescott of the Working Men's Club

As is customal at this time of the year, the vicar has asked me to step in and hold the fort, while he and his good lady go off on another of their many holidays!

Don't get me wrong. The vicar's earned every week he spends staying with his rich friends in their fancy palaces in Italy, Barbados and so forth.

Each to his own is what I say, and if you fancy having to sit round while some dodgy eyetie wearing a banana on his head does a cut-price imitation of a Neapolitan gondolier singing "Just One Cornetto", then good luck to you.

It may be the vicar's idea of a fun holiday, but some of us prefer to stay at home getting on with some real work!

No offence, your reverence, but while you've been swanning round the world's beaches free-of-charge (as of course you deserve after all the messes you've got us into in the past few months!), I have been quietly and modestly knuckling down to sorting a few thing out!

And firstly I'd like to thank the vicar's friend Mr Mandelson for not being here anymore, now that he's buggered off (excuse my Belgian!) to Brussels with his little foreign friend Reinaldo (no offence, Peter!), so that the rest of us can get on with our work without Mr Mandelson constantly sticking his nose in where it doesn't belong!

And secondly, it does not help when some prominent members of the PCC who are old enough to know better take it into their heads to start canoodling in the vestry with married ladies!

Not that it's anyone's business but Mr Blunkett's and that of the good lady in question, but what sort of example does it set, I ask, to the young folk in the parish?

I seem to remember the vicar and his pal Mr Campbell getting all high and mighty with Mr Cook when he was caught playing around in the organ loft with his little bit of fluff.

But now with Mr Blunkett it's a very different story – silence is golden and all that!

Perhaps it'll teach the vicar not to get on his high horse about what a good time we all had in the "Sixties"!

But the really important thing that I've managed to achieve in the vicar's absence, in case you missed it on the front page of the St Albion Mercury, is that I was able to rescue one of our parishioners who was literally "up the creek without a paddle"!

Remind you of anyone, Tony? (No offence, just a little joke to show that I'm not blowing my own trumpet!)

What happened was amazing! There was this bloke, just about to be swept to his doom in a raging torrent – and as he was pulled out by a couple of bystanders, I just happened to be there to have my photograph taken!

He was very grateful to me for my rescue and for the chance to see his picture in the papers under the headline "Super-Prezza To The Rescue!"

**SuperJohn to the rescue. By Mr de la Nougerede!**

Some of us, you see, like a bit of real adventure when we go on holiday, not just sitting around in Italy eating Valpolicelli and sucking up to blokes with bananas on their heads!

Get the picture?

Cheerio,

## John "Thunderbirds" Prescott

*(Holder of the Swimming Proficiency Certificate, Level 2: Life-saving skills!)*

# Postcard from the Vicar

Dear all,
Who says it's expensive in Italy since they brought in the Euro? We haven't spent a thing!
Love
Tony

# Thank you!

We are all very grateful to Mr Drayson for his wonderfully generous gift to parish funds. This has no connection with the fact that we have given him the contract to vaccinate all the kids in the parish. Another coincidence is that the vicar has put Mr Drayson's name forward to become a People's Peer, and that this was approved by return of post! Well done, Mr Drayson, and thanks a million – or rather half a million! T.B.

# Announcement

● Good News! The vicar has always been in favour of competitive sports and has decided to reintroduce the egg and spoon race at this year's village fete. It was cancelled last year on the grounds that the losing children might sue for compensation after suffering psychological trauma. How silly!

● Sorry! The egg and spoon race at this year's fete has unfortunately been cancelled due to the fact that the field where we used to run it has been sold and is now an executive housing development called "Prescott's Court"!

---

## A Message From Mr Milliband, Deputy Chair of Governors, St Albion Secondary School

*Congratulations to all the boys and girls of the school, every one of whom scored 100 percent in the recent A-level and GCSE exams, and some of them even more! So much for all those doom-merchants who whinge about falling standards! Stop trying to undermine our kids! It's time people gave praise where it's due – i.e. to the governors for changing the exam marking system so that every child gets a chance to shine! D.M.*

---

# ST ALBION PARISH NEWS

*17th September 2004*

*Hullo!*

Let me say straightaway that I have come back from my holidays firing on all cylinders and with my batteries fully recharged!

And, hey, don't we all feel the same sense of excitement, as we leave behind those long langorous weeks of lounging around Mr Berlusconi's pool and my good friend Cliff's private beach, and brace ourselves for all the challenges that autumn brings!

The kids are back at school. Everyone's back at work. There's a bracing nip in the air.

It's time for new ideas and new projects, and I can tell you, I've got plenty of them!

As my good friend the Rev. Dubya might put it, in his typical Texan way, "Hey, bud, let's go kick some ass!"

And there's no more visible sign that the parish is now moving into a new era than my decision to welcome back an old friend onto the PCC as my new right-hand man!

So, let's hear it for Mr Milburn! Stand up, Alan, so that the congregation can all remind themselves who you are!

As you all remember, only a year ago Alan came to me very regretfully, saying, "I'm sorry, Tony, to let you down badly, just when you needed me, but I've decided to put my family first, instead of my duty to the parish".

Of course, I was very understanding of Alan's dilemma. "I am a family man myself," I told him (although, unlike Mr Milburn, I am actually married!).

"No one understands better than me," I went on, "how difficult it is to combine working round the clock for our parish community with being a father and husband (or, in Mr Milburn's case, 'partner').

"But some of us," I had to tell him, "put the interests and needs of our fellow men and women first."

He, however, made a different choice, which he was perfectly entitled to do, even though he was wrong!

And at this point I wonder if any of the children remember the story of the so-called prodigal son?

Rashid? Vijay? No, well let me fill you in!

There was once a very foolish young man who decided to leave his best friend, to whom he owed everything, and travel far away into another land, to spend more time with his family.

And it didn't do him any good at all! He was very unhappy, far away from the centre of power, just moping around all day, watching afternoon TV and eating pork pies.

And then one day, it suddenly struck him that he was wasting his life, and that he needed to return to his friend and seek forgiveness.

Well, you can imagine how his friend might have felt when he saw the prodigal coming up the vicarage path and asking for his job back.

I can tell you that some people in that situation would have been very angry and told him in no uncertain terms to get lost!

But this friend (let's call him 'Tony'!) was not like that at all. He was full of compassion and fell upon the neck of his former colleague (not literally, of course – although there would be nothing wrong with that if it *had* been literally! We're a broad church, as Mr Mandelson and his partner Reinaldo would be the first to testify!).

No, this friend welcomed back the prodigal, saying to him, "Glad to have you back, Alan. You're just the man I need to help me with my new modernising initiatives. Bring that carrier bag of pork pies into the kitchen and we'll celebrate with a feast!"

But that's not the end of the story, is it, children? (Wake up, Rashid!)

No, there's another character, isn't there, whom we haven't mentioned so far, who's very important to the story (though not as important as he thinks he is!).

And that's the prodigal's older colleague who has stayed with the vicar, working dutifully night and day at his accounts!

When he sees the welcome given to the prodigal, he is furious.

"I've been loyal to you all these years, and yet I've never been given any pork pies or invited to a slap-up feast in the vicarage kitchen. This isn't fair!"

Now it was the vicar's turn to get angry! "You misunderstood everything, Gordon," he replied.

"Don't you know that there is more rejoicing in the vicarage when one of our disciples returns to the fold than there is when all the other gloomy Scottish sheep sit around muttering and moaning about how it is time for the shepherd to resign."

That's a 'parable', isn't it (a word we get from the Greek 'para', a load of, and 'ballos', wisdom).

I hope that'll give you all something to think about before our

'Service of Re-dedication' next week, for which, incidentally, I have written a special new chorus.

*Welcome home, welcome back,*
*Now we're really back on track.*
(Repeat)
*Alan-lulia, Alan-lulia.*

© Words and music, T. Blair.

Yours up for it!

*Tony*

---

# Who's Who
## The first in a series of one.
### First Lady of The Parish by Mary Ann Sieghart

I'd like you all to meet a very wonderful lady! She is not only a wonderful wife and mother, she is also the most successful career woman in the country, in her own right. She is ravishingly beautiful, dresses like a fashion model, with incredibly good taste, and does more for charity than Bob Geldof and Mother Teresa put together. Her vitality and charm enrich everyone who is privileged enough to meet her, whether it is in her exclusive Chambers, helping the under-privileged with their legal problems, or pouring out the coffee at the end of one of our morning services. And who is this saintly heroine of our time, with whom we are all profoundly honoured to breathe the same air? I am referring of course to Cherie Booth Q.C., our vicar's wife! *Mary Ann Seekjob*

---

# ▬ Vale ▬

Goodbye to Mr Smith, who has sadly had to resign from the PCC for "personal reasons". It would be inappropriate to spell out here what those "personal reasons" might be, but the fact that Mr Smith was about to be sacked must have preyed heavily on his mind, possibly leading him to become severely depressed and in urgent need of professional psychiatric help. We'd like to thank Alan for whatever it was he did, (although I gather he left quite a bit to be desired in the way he carried out his work!). We wish him all luck for the future, and a speedy recovery from his tragic breakdown! T.B.

# ✉ Parish Postbag

*Dear Sir*

*In reply to the vicar's request to be supplied with more detailed information about the parish accounts, may I remind you that I am a busy man and I don't have time to give valuable data to financial illiterates like the vicar who*

> *Yours faithfully*
> *Gordon Brown*
> *Parish Treasurer and*
> *Vicar-in-waiting*

**The vicar regrets that some letters may have to be cut for reasons of space, as might some jobs such as Parish Treasurer, if people don't watch out. T.B.**

# Final Thought[*]

**Ask not for whom the bell tolls...
Because it's not for me!**

*Don't get excited, Gordon, it's only the end of the *book*!